THE GOURMET'S GUIDE TO
COOKING WITH
CHOCOLATE

QUARRY

First published in the United States of America by
Quarry Books, a member of
Quayside Publishing Group
100 Cummings Center
Suite 406-L
Beverly, Massachusetts 01915-6101
Telephone: (978) 282-9590
Fax: (978) 283-2742
www.quarrybooks.com

Library of Congress Cataloging-in-Publication Data
Ridgaway, Dwayne.
   The gourmet's guide to cooking with chocolate : how to use chocolate to take simple recipes from the ordinary to the extraordinary / Dwayne Ridgaway.
      p. cm.
   Includes index.
   ISBN-13: 978-1-59253-592-7
   ISBN-10: 1-59253-592-5
   1. Cookery (Chocolate) 2. Chocolate desserts. I. Title.
   TX767.C5R57 2010
   641.3'374--dc22

                                                         2009031114
                                                              CIP

ISBN-13978-1-59253-592-7
ISBN-10: 1-59253-592-5

10 9 8 7 6 5 4 3 2 1

Page Layout: Claire MacMaster, barefoot art graphic design
Photography: Glenn Scott
Food Styling: Catrine Kelty
Cover Image: Rockport Publishers

Printed in China

THE GOURMET'S GUIDE TO

COOKING WITH

CHOCOLATE

How to Use Chocolate to Take Simple Recipes from the Ordinary to the Extraordinary

BEVERLY MASSACHUSETTS

QUARRY BOOKS

DWAYNE RIDGAWAY

Contents

Introduction

crave [krāv]: to long for, want greatly or desire eagerly

We can crave many things—the latest fashions, the newest car, the best wine—but what more powerful craving is there than that for chocolate? The mere sound of the word elicits cravings. Is it simply flavor, hormones, or a chemical in our brain?

Perusing the contents of this book might find you with a hankering for a glass of chocolate milk, or a single, decadent truffle. How many times have you found yourself passing by a candy shop, window displays brimming with little confections that pull you in, inevitably causing you to buy something?

There are many answers to questions about cravings ranging from the scientifically sound to the philosophical, but this is not a medical journal or a research paper. It is, however, a collection of 150 delicious ways to satisfy the craving.

This book aspires to take the mystery out of cooking and baking with chocolate and make it a pleasure. Having attended culinary school, I have seen some remarkable achievements in chocolate, including cakes and candies that are more like sculpture than food. Those are the extremes; here we take a simpler approach to creating with chocolate. We explore the nature of chocolate and why certain types are better for a recipe than others.

Where Chocolate Comes From

Chocolate begins as fruit from the cacao tree. Thought to have originated in the Amazon River Basin, cacao trees are a tropical plant growing along what is known as the "chocolate belt" or the tropical band that extends twenty degrees north and south of the equator.

The Gourmet's Guide to the Essentials of Chocolate

Major chocolate-producing countries are found across the globe:

Latin America: Belize, Bolivia, Brazil, Costa Rica, El Salvador, and Grenada
Asia: Fiji, India, Malaysia, the Philippines, and Vietnam
Africa: Ghana, Madagascar, Nigeria, and Tanzania

The four species of cacao trees are Forastero, Criollo, Trinitario, and Nacional. Each tree produces either bulk (ordinary) or flavor (fine) beans. Most scientific studies point to Forastero as the original species of cacao. Forastero beans are classified as bulk beans, and they make up more than 95 percent of the world's crop. They are high-yielding trees that produce a crop for more years than the other species, and their pods have a robust flavor. Criollo trees produce what is considered a flavor bean, lending more delicate qualities to chocolate. Criollo trees are harder to grow, and yield fewer pods. The Trinitario, named for its development in Trinidad, is a hybrid species. A combination of the Criollo and Forastero. It is also considered a fine chocolate flavor-producing species. The Nacional species is native to Ecuador. It is a variation of the Forastero bean with many traits of the Criollo bean, and thus considered a flavor bean.

The cacao beans grow in pods. When harvested, the beans are removed from the pods and sent through a process that includes fermenting, sun-drying, roasting, and then ultimately breaking into nibs. These nibs are then ground to a paste. During this process, some of the cocoa butter (natural fat) is removed. The end result is a dark, bitter, paste called cocoa liquor, also unsweetened or bitter-sweet chocolate. Sugars, condensed milk, or milk solids are added to this liquor to make a variety of chocolate.

Types of Chocolate

Everyone's tastes differ, and everyone's palate will interpret a type of chocolate differently. Most of the recipes in this book use semisweet and bittersweet chocolate interchanageably.

DARK CHOCOLATE

Containing 50 to 90 percent cocoa liquor and little or no milk products, dark chocolate has little to no sweetness. The higher the percentage of cocoa liquor, the less sweet the chocolate. Some dark chocolate, depending on the manufacturer, may have added sugar to give it a more palatable sweetness. Both semisweet and bittersweet refer to dark chocolate, but semisweet simply has more added sugar.

MILK CHOCOLATE

The most popular eating chocolate, milk chocolate is made of pure chocolate with added cocoa butter, sugar, and milk solids. It is most commonly sold as candy bars and chocolate chips. It can be used in place of dark chocolate in most recipes, but it has a lighter, sweeter taste than good-quality dark chocolate.

COCOA POWDER

Commonly used in baking or creating hot chocolate beverages, unsweetened cocoa powder is simply defatted pure chocolate. Most of the cocoa butter has been removed, and the remaining chocolate solids are ground into unsweetened cocoa powder. Dutch-process cocoa powder is treated with alkali, making it less bitter. It is recommended in most baking because of its milder flavor.

WHITE CHOCOLATE

What we know as white chocolate in the baking aisle is really not chocolate at all. Often referred to as confectionery coating, white chocolate contains cocoa butter, milk solids, sugar, and vanilla for flavor. It is very sweet and creamy, lacking any bitterness that a dark chocolate would have. White chocolate behaves differently than dark chocolate when cooking or baking; the core ingredients are different and often can't be substituted for chocolate in recipes.

COUVERTURE

Artisans in the chocolate-making field know this as "coating choco-

Chocolate in Profile

Bitter or Semisweet Chocolate	Bitter or semisweet chocolate may or may not have added sugar; the bitterness is primarily a result of roasting. The more heavily roasted a bean is the more bitter the taste.
White Chocolate	White chocolate has no cocoa solids, just cocoa butter. Because of this, chocolate purists will say that white chocolate is not chocolate at all but a confection.
Milk Chocolate	Milk chocolate is cocoa liquor with added sugar and dairy (milk, cream, milk powder, or condensed milk). By (U.S.) law milk chocolate must contain little or no less than 10% cocoa liquor (by weight), 3.3% milk fat, and 12% milk solids.
Dark Chocolate	Any chocolate that contains no milk; some processed dark chocolates may contain dairy products.

late." It is made distinct by its higher cocoa butter content. It is a dark chocolate that melts exceptionally well, and is typically used by candy makers for dipping and enrobing cakes, candies, and pastries.

COCOA NIBS

Relatively new to the chocolate scene, cocoa nibs are roasted, hulled, and broken cacao beans. Found in gourmet shops and baking boutiques, nibs have an intense flavor, a delicate crunch, and a unique texture making them quite versatile to cook with. They appear in several recipes in this book. Whether ground, crushed, or used as is, they add flavor to many dishes.

Essentials of Selecting Chocolates

The best place to find good-quality chocolates is the candy aisle of the supermarket. Lately, candy shelves have exploded with gourmet, small batch, and select chocolates from every major manufacturer. If you are lucky enough to have gourmet grocers in your area, you will find that their selection of chocolates (from baking chocolate to flavored and infused) is even finer.

Higher-quality brands that were used extensively in recipe-testing for this book are Lindt, Scharffen Berger, Ghirardelli, Dagoba, Valrhona, and Callebaut. Treat yourself to several bars from different manufacturers to determine which ones you prefer before baking.

Overview of Chocolate Manufacturing

Between cacao bean and chocolate bar, there is a standard manufacturing process that all beans go through.

HARVESTING

Harvesting remains a manual process, due to the fragile nature of the stem and flower cushions of the tree. A stem or flower cushion damaged during harvest will never bear fruit again. Likewise, a damaged pod is susceptible to disease and rot. The seeds must be removed from the pod by mallet or machete within a few hours to a couple of days. The average mature cacao tree can produce 5 to 6 pounds (2.3 to 2.7 kg) of dried cocoa beans annually.

PROCESSING: FERMENTATION AND DRYING

Fermentation has tremendous influence on the flavors in chocolate. For the chocolate flavors to fully develop the seeds must go through a two-step fermentation process: anaerobic (the absence of air) and aerobic (with air). Fermentation lasts between three and seven days and is dependent on the type of seed, quantity of seeds, the chosen method, and the difference in day and night temperatures.

The goal of drying is to reduce the moisture content of the beans to about 7 percent. This can take as long as a week (weather conditions pending) since drying is done primarily by the Sun. As with fermentation, the drying process is an important step in the development of flavors in chocolate.

SELECTING

Through what is called a cut test, random beans are selected from a batch and cut before being graded. During this grading the selector is assessing the following qualities: proper fermentation; the average weight of the bean; bean defects such as insect damage, flat and small beans, and germinated beans.

MANUFACTURING

Most manufacturing plants run cacao beans through the following steps:

- Cleaning and sanitizing to rid the beans of foreign objects and micro-organisms
- Roasting the beans at low temperatures for longer periods of time, depending on the type of bean and the type of chocolate being made
- After roasting, the beans are winnowed: The meat or nibs of the bean are released from the shell and separated. The nibs are then ground to a paste known as the cocoa liquor. (Cocoa liquor, in its simplest form is unsweetened or bittersweet chocolate.)
- Conching, the final step, is stirring the chocolate at a low heat for several hours or even days. Conching aids in the evaporation of excess moisture in the chocolate, yielding a smoother, more velvety product. In general, the finer the chocolate, the longer the conching process. Cocoa butter and/or lecithin may be added to thin the chocolate for molding.

Understanding Gourmet Chocolate: Percentages and Origins

Labels on chocolate bars have begun to look as complex as wine labels. Many manufacturers are prominently featuring a percentage on the label, which represents the amount of ground cacao beans and cocoa butter in the chocolate versus the sugar and other ingredients. The higher the percentage, the more bitter the chocolate.

Some chocolates boast the terms single-origin, plantation, or vintage. These terms refer to a chocolate having been made from the cacao bean of a single country, region, or plantation, much like a fine wine or coffee bean. Most chocolates are a blend of beans from a variety of locations. Single-origin or plantation chocolates can take on the characteristics of the land and soil from which they are grown. Labels aside, remember that using high-quality chocolate will achieve a high-quality result.

When determining the quality of a chocolate to be used for a recipe, consider the role or the intensity of the chocolate in the dish. If you are baking cookies that have five other ingredients all contributing characteristic flavors to the cookie, then the chocolate is not necessarily the star. Indulge in a high-quality fine chocolate when making a soufflé or mousse in which the entire satisfaction of the dish is in the quality of the chocolate.

A Guide to Working with Chocolate

Chocolate can be temperamental, but there is no reason to be intimidated by it. Always store it properly, melt it with caution, use good quality chocolate for good quality results, and explore your available options. The rest is just simple cooking and baking.

STORING CHOCOLATE

Proper chocolate storage will ensure it has a long, natural shelf life. Blooming is the graying that appears on the surface of chocolate, indicating changes in temperature during storage. Blooming does not affect the chocolate's taste or quality, but it may make you question it. To prevent blooming, store chocolate in a cool, dry place but not in the refrigerator. Chocolate is also susceptible to absorbing odors, so store it in airtight containers or zippered storage bags.

GRATING AND CHOPPING CHOCOLATE

Sometimes a recipe calls for grating or chopping chocolate. Grating the chocolate allows it to melt faster or incorporate easier into a dish. When melting chocolate for a recipe, chopping usually suffices. The finer the chop, the quicker the chocolate will melt. Grating tip: If using grated chocolate as a finishing touch on top of a dish, freeze the chocolate for about 15 minutes beforehand. It will grate more coarsely than if it were at room temperature.

MELTING CHOCOLATE

Melting chocolate requires a few simple guidelines:

Chocolate will scorch. You don't want chocolate to come into direct contact with a heat source or the bottom of a pan. A double boiler is preferred for melting chocolate.

Chocolate reacts to liquid in odd ways. If there is not enough liquid to absorb the fats in the chocolate, the chocolate mixture will become solid and grainy. When melting chocolate with no added liquid, do not allow any water or moisture into it. The tiniest drop of moisture will wreak havoc on the chocolate, causing it to seize. If it seizes, the chocolate may be unusable.

If your chocolate seizes, try mixing a small amount of vegetable or canola oil with the chocolate to make it smooth again. A small amount of oil will not affect a recipe. If this trick does not work, you will need to discard the seized chocolate and start with new.

Chocolate can also be melted in a microwave; however, the double-boiler method is easier to monitor and control during the process.

MELTING CHOCOLATE IN A DOUBLE BOILER

If you do not have a true double boiler, place a glass or stainless-steel bowl over a pot of boiling water.

1. To melt the chocolate quickly, chop or grate it first. For chopping, use a sharp chef's knife or serrated knife. For grating, use a micro-plane. Or, if appropriate for the recipe, use chocolate chips.

2. Fill a saucepan with about 2" (5.1 cm) of water and bring to a slow boil over medium heat. Place the top of the double boiler, or the heatproof bowl that fits snugly, over the saucepan of boiling water.

3. Do not cover the bowl. This will create steam, the water from which will ruin the chocolate. Don't allow the water in the sauce pan to touch the bowl with the chocolate as this may create moisture on the inside of the bowl.

4. Once the chocolate has started to melt, remove the double boiler from the heat, stirring the chocolate gently until melted.

MICROWAVE MELTING

The microwave can is a good way to melt chocolate quickly if you pay close attention during the process.

1. Follow step 1 for Melting Chocolate in a Double Boiler, above.

2. Place the chopped chocolate or chips in a microwave-safe bowl, uncovered.

3. Use the microwave on medium or low power to prevent scorching the chocolate.

4. Stir with every 15 seconds during the heating process until the chocolate is completely melted. The amount of time it takes to melt depends on the amount of chocolate you are melting. You can melt any quantity in one bowl; just remember to stir every 15 seconds.

1

Candies, Bars, and Cookies

White Chocolate Lemon Cheesecake Bars with Vanilla Wafer Crust

The lemon is a fresh, clean counterpoint to the sweet vanilla crust. Consider baking these in a shallow baking dish, then cutting them into bars or squares. They can be served as a finger dessert instead of a traditional slice of cheesecake.

1½	cups (180 g) ground vanilla wafers
½	cup (50 g) ground almonds
½	cup (112 g) unsalted butter, melted
1½	cups (300 g) granulated sugar
3	(8-ounce, or 225 g) packages cream cheese, softened
4	ounces (115 g) white chocolate, melted
4	large eggs
½	cup (115 g) sour cream
1½	teaspoons grated lemon zest
3	tablespoons (45 ml) fresh lemon juice

Preheat oven to 350°F (180°C, or gas mark 4). Spray a 9 × 13-inch (22.5 × 32.5 cm) baking dish with nonstick cooking spray. Combine the ground vanilla wafers, ground almonds, melted butter, and ¼ cup (50 g) sugar in a mixing bowl. Pour into prepared pan and press into the bottom and up the sides. Bake for 8 minutes, remove, and cool.

In the bowl of a stand mixer fitted with the paddle attachment, combine the cream cheese, melted white chocolate and 1¼ cups (250 g) sugar, beat until smooth and creamy, about 3 minutes. Add the eggs one at a time, beating to combine after each addition. Add the sour cream, lemon zest, and lemon juice, beat to combine. Pour mixture into prepared crust and bake for 45 to 60 minutes, until set and firm.

Remove from the oven and run knife around edges to release crust from sides of pan. Allow to cool completely on a wire rack. Cover with plastic wrap and refrigerate for at least 4 hours to firm up. Cut into squares and serve.

Prep = 30 minutes   **Cook** = 45 to 60 minutes
Chill = 4 hours   **Yield** = 20 squares

Chocolate-Pretzel Clusters

Chocolate-covered pretzels should be standard in everyone's chocolate repertoire, and this recipe takes them up a notch. The pretzels mix perfectly with other favorite salty snacks—peanuts and popcorn—especially when everything is coated with chocolate.

- 12 ounces (340 g) semisweet chocolate chips or chunks, chopped (about 1$\frac{1}{2}$ cups)
- $\frac{1}{4}$ teaspoon vanilla extract
- 1 cup (150 g) broken pretzel sticks
- 1$\frac{1}{2}$ cups (220 g) salted dry-roasted peanuts
- 6 cups (50 g) popped lightly salted or kettle-cooked popcorn

Melt the chocolate in the top part of a double boiler, or in a stainless-steel mixing bowl set over a pan of barely simmering water. Once melted, remove from heat. Stir in the vanilla extract. Add the pretzels, peanuts, and popcorn, stirring to coat evenly. Spread mixture on a waxed paper-lined sheet pan. Cover with plastic wrap and refrigerate until hardened, about 1 hour. When ready to serve, break apart into clumps.

Prep = 15 minutes **Chill** = 1 hour **Yield** = 10 servings

Brutti ma Buoni Cookies

Translated, *brutti ma buoni* means "ugly but good." On a recent trip to Italy, a friend raved about these chocolate delights, which are a popular Italian treat. A number of traditional recipes call for a combination of hazelnuts, almonds, and pine nuts, with a hint of cocoa and egg whites for crispness. My version aspires to reach the level of "dessert classic."

1/2	cup (58 g) chopped hazelnuts
1/3	cup (40 g) chopped almonds
1/4	cup (35 g) pine nuts
5	egg whites, at room temperature
1	cup (200 g) granulated sugar
1/4	cup (30 g) all-purpose flour
1	tablespoon (15 ml) pure vanilla extract
1	tablespoon (15 ml) Frangelico (or other hazelnut liqueur)
	Zest of 1 orange, grated finely
1 1/2	tablespoons (9 g) unsweetened cocoa powder

Preheat the oven to 325°F (170°C, or gas mark 3). Place hazelnuts, almonds, and pine nuts on a baking sheet and bake for 7 minutes, until toasted and aromatic. Butter a cookie sheet and dust with flour. Place the egg whites in the bowl of a stand mixer fitted with the whisk attachment. Whip until soft peaks form. Gradually add the sugar and beat 2 minutes. Add the flour, vanilla, Frangelico, orange zest, and cocoa. Blend 1 minute; stir in the nuts by hand. Spoon the batter in 2-inch (5 cm) mounds 2 inches (5 cm) apart on the cookie sheet. Bake 25 to 30 minutes, until crisp. Transfer to wire racks to cool completely; store in an airtight container.

Prep = 30 minutes   **Cook** = 25 minutes   **Yield** = 3 dozen cookies

Browned Butter Short-bread with Pistachios and White Chocolate

Browning butter is a process that separates the solids from the melted liquid, essentially toasting the solids at the same time. This technique gives the butter a robust quality that adds depth to these shortbreads.

2   sticks (225 g) butter
1½ cups (180 g) all-purpose flour
¼   cup (33 g) cornstarch
¼   teaspoon fine sea salt
½   teaspoon black pepper
¾   cup (175 g) firmly packed brown sugar
2   teaspoons vanilla extract
1   teaspoon orange zest
½   cup (70 g) finely chopped pistachios

WHITE CHOCOLATE-ORANGE GLAZE:
8   ounces (225 g) white chocolate, chopped
½   teaspoon orange extract

In a small saucepan over medium heat, melt the butter until the solids are separated and beginning to brown. Turn off the heat and stir—do not burn the butter. Set aside and allow to cool for 2 minutes. Pour the liquid butter into a dish, leaving the solids in the pan. Set the butter aside.

Once the butter has solidified, continue. Sift the flour, cornstarch, salt, and black pepper in a bowl. Using a mixer and paddle attachment, beat the butter with the brown sugar on medium speed until smooth, about 3 minutes. Add the vanilla extract and orange zest and beat to combine. Reduce the speed to low and add the dry ingredients one cup at a time, mixing just to combine. Do not overmix. Add the pistachios and beat just to incorporate.

Scrape the dough from the bowl onto a waxed paper-lined sheet pan. Shape dough into an 8-inch (20 cm) square about ¼ inch (0.6 cm) thick. Cover with plastic wrap and refrigerate for at least 2 hours.

To Bake: Preheat the oven to 350°F (180°C, or gas mark 4). Cut dough into 12 squares. Transfer squares to a sheet pan and pierce each square a few times with a fork. Place on the middle rack of the oven and bake for 15 minutes, until just turning brown. Remove from oven and allow to cool on the sheet pan until firm. (Right out of the oven, the shortbreads will be crumbly and tend to fall apart.)

For the White Chocolate-Orange Glaze: Melt the chocolate in a double boiler. Add the orange extract, stirring to combine. Dip each cookie in the chocolate or drizzle in a fine stream over the cookies.

Prep = 30 minutes **Cook** = 15 minutes **Chill** = 2 hours
Yield = 1 dozen cookies

Chocolate Baklava

From Russia with love comes this classic baklava recipe with a touch of chocolate. This recipe has been in my mother's recipe drawer for years and has always been a hit. I updated it by adding dark chocolate to the syrup and topping the whole pan with drizzled melted chocolate for a beautiful finish.

    1   pound (455 g) butter
    1   pound (455 g) phyllo pastry
    8   ounces (225 g) ground pecans and walnuts mixed together
    1   pound (455 g) dark chocolate, melted

SYRUP:
    3   cups (600 g) granulated sugar
    2   cups (475 ml) water
        Juice of ½ lemon
    2   cinnamon sticks
    3   tablespoons (60 g) honey

To clarify butter, place in a saucepan over medium heat, allow to melt, and cook until the foamy white solids rise to the top. Spoon away the foamy solids and discard. What remains is clarified butter.

Preheat oven to 375°F (190°C, or gas mark 5). Brush bottom and sides of a 9 × 13-inch (22.5 × 32.5 cm) baking pan with melted butter.

When working with the phyllo sheets, use a damp kitchen towel to cover the sheets you aren't using. This prevents them from drying out and becoming brittle. Layer the bottom of the prepared pan with 6 sheets of pastry, brushing each completely with clarified butter before layering on the next sheet. Sprinkle last buttered sheet with one-fifth of the nuts and drizzle with chocolate. Layer two sheets of pastry, again brushing each with butter. Layer with two more sheets of pastry brushed with butter and then nuts and chocolate. Repeat until five layers of nuts and chocolate are complete. Reserve remaining chocolate to garnish tops. Top with the remaining seven or eight sheets of phyllo that are left, buttering each one individually. Using a very sharp knife, cut pastry into diamond-shaped pieces, cutting only halfway through the pastry. Brush top with butter. Place in oven and bake at 375°F (190°C, or gas mark 5) for 12 minutes, then lower the temperature to 350°F (180°C, or gas mark 4) and bake for 30 to 40 minutes, until golden brown. Remove from oven and cool for 10 minutes.

Prepare the syrup: While the baklava is baking, bring sugar, water, lemon juice, and cinnamon sticks to a boil; reduce heat; and simmer to a thick syrup, about 25 to 30 minutes. Add honey and continue to simmer for 10 more minutes. Transfer to a wire rack to cool. Remove the cinnamon stick before pouring over baklava. Always use cool syrup over hot baklava.

Pour cooled syrup over hot baklava. Let sit for several hours before cutting pastry through to bottom; this will allow syrup to drain through all the layers. Once cut through, drizzle the reserved chocolate over the top, creating a crisscrossing effect. It is best to let set overnight before serving. Cover loosely with plastic wrap.

Prep = 30 minutes   **Cook** = 42 to 52 minutes   **Chill** = Overnight
Yield = About 32 pieces

Triple Chocolate Pecan Clusters

These smart little clusters take just minutes to make and are a great snack to have around the house. If pecans aren't your favorite, try cashews, almonds, or peanuts (or all three) as an alternative. Unsweetened chocolate can be used in place of peanut butter chips, too. (If starting with a bar or square of chocolate, chop it before melting.)

4	ounces (115 g) white chocolate
$1/2$	cup (88 g) milk chocolate chips
6	ounces (170 g) semisweet chocolate, chopped
$1/2$	cup (88 g) peanut butter baking chips
$1\frac{1}{2}$	cups (165 g) pecans, toasted
$3/4$	cup (64 g) dried coconut

Prepare a double boiler over high heat. Place all the chocolates and the peanut butter chips in the top of the double boiler and melt, stirring occasionally. Add the pecans and coconut, stirring to coat and combine.

Using two tablespoons, drop spoonfuls of the mixture onto a waxed paper-lined sheet pan. Cover loosely with plastic wrap and refrigerate until hardened, about 1 hour.

Prep = 10 minutes **Chill** = 1 hour
Yield = 8 to 10 servings

Raspberry Pecan Truffles

Decadent and luscious, these truffles are bursting with the flavor of raspberries. Using raspberry preserves adds natural texture to the truffles because of the seeds. If you prefer a more subtle, smooth result, use raspberry jam instead.

8 ounces (225 g) semisweet chocolate chips or chunks, chopped
1/3 cup (75 g) butter
1/3 cup (107 g) raspberry preserves
1/2 cup (55 g) chopped pecans, toasted
1/4 teaspoon vanilla extract
2 tablespoons (28 ml) tawny port wine

1 cup (110 g) finely chopped pecans or
1/4 cup (23 g) cocoa powder, sifted

In the top of a double boiler, melt the chocolate with the butter, stirring with a wooden spoon until smooth. Add raspberry preserves, pecans, vanilla extract, and port; stir to combine. Pour the chocolate into a shallow container and refrigerate until cooled completely (at least 2 hours). Scoop out chocolate using either a tablespoon or a small (1-ounce, or 28 g) ice-cream scoop. Gently roll the scoops into balls and roll in chopped pecans or cocoa powder.

To toast the pecans: spread out evenly on a sheet pan. Place on center rack of oven and bake at 350°F (180°C, or gas mark 4) for 12 minutes, until pecans begin to brown and an aromatic smell develops. Do not overcook, as the nuts will continue to toast a bit while cooling. Remove from the oven and allow to cool.

Prep = 10 minutes **Total Time** = 2 hours 20 minutes
Yield = About 24 truffles

Classic Chocolate Truffles

Truffles are a classic chocolate recipe. Simple to make, elegant in presentation, and decadent in taste—truffles are a great have-around-the-house chocolate delight.

4 tablespoons (½ stick, or 55 g) unsalted butter
8 ounces (225 g) semisweet chocolate chips or squares, chopped
¼ cup (60 ml) heavy cream
¼ teaspoon vanilla extract
  Confectioners' sugar or unsweetened cocoa powder, sifted, for dusting

In the top bowl of a double boiler, melt the butter and the chocolate with the heavy cream; add vanilla extract and stir to combine. Pour the chocolate into a container and refrigerate until completely cooled (at least 2 hours). Scoop chocolate out using either a tablespoon or a small (1-ounce, or 28 g) ice-cream scoop. Gently roll the scoops into balls and dust with confectioners' sugar or cocoa powder.

Clockwise from top: Espresso-Nut Truffles, page 26; confectioners' sugar and cocoa powder variations of Classic Chocolate Truffles

Prep = 10 minutes **Total Time** = 2 hours 20 minutes
Yield = About 24 truffles

Espresso-Nut Truffles

A simple espresso twist updates the classic chocolate truffle. The rich taste of chocolate pairs perfectly with the mellow depth of espresso.

- 4 tablespoons (½ stick, or 55 g) unsalted butter
- 8 ounces (225 g) semisweet chocolate chips or squares, chopped
- ¼ cup (60 ml) heavy cream
- ¼ teaspoon vanilla extract
- ¼ cup (60 ml) coffee liqueur (such as Kahlua)
- 1 tablespoon (6 g) instant espresso powder dissolved in 1 teaspoon hot water
- Cocoa powder or confectioners' sugar, sifted, for dusting

In the top of a double boiler, melt the butter and the chocolate with the heavy cream. Add vanilla extract, coffee liqueur, and espresso; stir to combine. Pour the chocolate into a container and refrigerate until cooled completely (at least 2 hours). Scoop out chocolate using either a tablespoon or a small (1-ounce, [28 g]) ice-cream scoop. Gently roll the scoops into balls and dust with cocoa powder or confectioners' sugar.

Prep = 10 minutes **Total Time** = 2 hours 20 minutes
Yield = About 24 truffles

Green Tea Truffles with Bay Essence

Green tea is a great flavor for infusing into many applications. Here, I have enhanced it with the scent of bay leaves to make truffles with an exotic flavor. Use fresh or good-quality dried bay leaves for the best flavor, and any green tea you prefer. I chose to use pure green tea with no fruit flavoring to keep the flavor simple and clean.

- 1/4 cup (60 ml) heavy cream
- 1 tea bag green tea
- 2 bay leaves, bruised
- 4 tablespoons (1/2 stick, or 55 g) unsalted butter
- 4 ounces (115 g) semisweet chocolate chips or squares, chopped
- 4 ounces (115 g) milk chocolate chips
- 1/4 teaspoon vanilla extract
  Cocoa powder for dusting
  Confectioners' sugar, for dusting

In a saucepan over medium heat, warm the heavy cream with the tea bag and the bay leaves until bubbles form around the edges. Remove from heat and let steep for 30 minutes. Remove tea bag and squeeze all the liquid out; remove the bay leaves. Return the cream to the heat to warm again just until bubbles form around the edges. In the top bowl of a double boiler, melt the butter and the chocolates until smooth. Remove from heat and pour in the warm cream and the vanilla, stirring until smooth. Pour the chocolate into a container and refrigerate until cooled completely (at least 2 hours). Scoop out chocolate using either a tablespoon or a small (1-ounce [28 g]) ice-cream scoop. Gently roll the scoops into balls and dust with cocoa powder or confectioners' sugar.

Prep = 10 minutes **Total Time** = 2 hours 20 minutes
Yield = About 24 truffles

Italian Bigne with Chocolate Pastry Cream (St. Joseph's Day Pastries)

St. Joseph's Day Pastries are an Italian staple in dessert shops. These are a classic recipe filled with a rich and creamy Italian Chocolate Pastry Cream.

1¼   cups (295 ml) water
³⁄₄   cup (90 g) flour
5   tablespoons (70 g) butter
4   eggs
1   teaspoon lemon extract
1   tablespoon (15 ml) vanilla extract
1   teaspoon lemon zest
      Oil, for baking sheet
      Confectioners' sugar, for dusting

In a medium pot, bring the water to a boil over high heat. When the water boils, remove the pan from the heat and add all of the flour, stirring immediately until smooth. Add the butter and return the pan to medium heat, stirring until combined. The flour mixture will form a ball. Stir until the dough pulls away from the sides of the pan. Remove from the heat and allow to cool. Add eggs one at a time, stirring after each addition until completely incorporated into the pastry. Stir in the lemon and vanilla extracts and the lemon zest. Let the batter rest for at least 15 minutes. Using a soup spoon, place spoonfuls of batter on a greased cookie sheet. Leave at least 2 inches (5.1 cm) between the drops. Bake at 400°F (200°C, or gas mark 6) for 10 minutes. Reduce the heat to 375°F (190°C, or gas mark 5) and bake for another 15 to 20 minutes, until the pastries are golden brown. Turn the oven off and let the pastries dry in the oven. Don't remove until they are completely cool. Gently open and fill each pastry with Italian Chocolate Pastry Cream—recipe follows. Dust the tops with confectioners' sugar.

Prep = 20 minutes **Cook** = 30 minutes **Chill** = 2 hours
Yield = 2 dozen pastries

Italian Chocolate Pastry Cream

Use this as a filling for the St. Joseph's Day Pastries (page 28).

5	tablespoons (63 g) granulated sugar
5	egg yolks, at room temperature
5	tablespoons (38 g) all-purpose flour
2¾	cups (645 ml) whole milk
1¼	teaspoons vanilla extract
1	teaspoon orange extract
½	cup (88 g) chopped dark chocolate

Place the sugar, egg yolks, and flour in a medium saucepan. Stir, using a wooden spoon, until the sugar is dissolved. In a separate saucepan, heat the milk over medium heat just until steaming—a thin film will form over the top (do not allow to boil). Place the egg mixture over medium heat and gradually pour the milk mixture over the egg mixture, stirring constantly with a whisk. Cook the mixture until it just reaches the boiling point. Add the vanilla and orange extracts. Lower the heat and continue to cook for about 4 minutes, stirring constantly. Add the chocolate and stir to incorporate. The pastry cream will have the consistency of pudding. Remove from heat, and place a piece of waxed paper on the surface of the pastry cream to prevent a skin from forming. Allow it to cool to room temperature, about 4 hours, before filling the Italian Bigne.

Prep = 15 minutes   **Chill** = 4 hours
Yield = About 3 cups cream

Pastry Shop Brownies

The best bakeries are often the ones who make the simplest, most delicious brownies—and they know how to ply you with piles of the decadent treat. No fuss, no muss, without a lot of extras: perfect brownies are a pure celebration of chocolate. These are of that tradition: fudgy and cakey with a pow of chocolate.

- 6 ounces (170 g) dark chocolate, chopped
- 1/2 cup (1 stick, or 112 g) unsalted butter, softened
- 1 cup (200 g) sugar
  Pinch salt
- 2 eggs, at room temperature
- 1/2 teaspoon pure vanilla extract
- 1/2 cup (60 g) all-purpose flour
- 1/3 cup (30 g) unsweetened cocoa powder
- 1/2 cup chopped walnuts, toasted

Preheat oven to 325°F (170°C, or gas mark 3). Grease an 8-inch square baking pan with nonstick cooking spray. Line with two sheets of parchment paper that overhang the sides of the pan, acting as handles with which to remove the brownies. Melt the chocolate in the top of a double boiler and set aside. In the bowl of a stand mixer fitted with the paddle attachment, beat the butter with the sugar until smooth. Add the salt, eggs, cooled melted chocolate, and vanilla, and beat just to combine. Add the flour and cocoa powder, beating just to incorporate. Mix in the nuts by hand. Pour batter into prepared pan and bake on the middle rack of the oven for 25 to 30 minutes, until brownies are firm and the sides begin to pull away from the pan. Remove from the oven and let cool 10 minutes. Remove the brownies from pan using parchment "handles," and cut into squares.

Prep = 20 minutes   **Cook** = 25 minutes   **Chill** = 20 minutes
Yield = 16 brownies

Peanut Butter Marbled Brownies

As every candy-bar lover knows, chocolate and peanut butter are a perfect pair.

4 ounces (115 g) dark chocolate chips or squares, chopped
2 ounces (55 g) milk chocolate chips or squares, chopped
1/2 cup (1 stick, or 112 g) unsalted butter, softened
1 cup (200 g) granulated sugar
1/4 teaspoon salt
2 eggs, at room temperature
1/2 teaspoon pure vanilla extract
1/2 cup (60 g) all-purpose flour
1/3 cup (90 g) unsweetened cocoa powder

PEANUT BUTTER FILLING:
4 tablespoons (55 g) unsalted butter, melted
1/2 cup (50 g) confectioners' sugar
3/4 cup (195 g) smooth peanut butter
1/4 teaspoon salt
1/2 teaspoon pure vanilla extract

Preheat oven to 325°F (170°C, or gas mark 3). Grease an 8-inch (20 cm) square baking pan with nonstick cooking spray. Line with two sheets of parchment paper that overhang the sides of the pan. Melt the chocolates in the bowl of a double boiler, set aside. With stand mixer and paddle, beat the butter with the sugar until smooth. Add the salt, eggs, cooled melted chocolate, and vanilla, and beat just to combine. Add the flour and cocoa, beating just to incorporate.

Prepare the filling: In a small bowl, stir together the butter, confectioners' sugar, peanut butter, salt, and vanilla until smooth. Pour half the brownie batter into the prepared pan. Spoon dollops of the peanut butter filling randomly on top of batter. Pour remaining batter on top, spreading in an even layer. Dollop remaining peanut butter filling on top. Run a butter knife through dollops, leaving a marbled effect. Bake on middle rack of oven for about 45 minutes, until a wooden skewer inserted in the middle comes out clean. Let cool in the pan for 15 minutes, then transfer out of pan to a rack, allowing to cool completely before cutting into squares.

Prep = 20 minutes **Cook** = 45 minutes **Yield** = 16 brownies

Golden Rocky Road Fudge

Fudge is a classic candy that evokes memories of boardwalk candy shop windows—summertime seashore vacation spots, arcade games, amusement rides, and enough confections to feed an army. Rocky road, the blend of velvety chocolate with marshmallows and nuts, is a staple on the fudge-shop menu. I have added dried cranberries and golden raisins for a sweet and tart twist on the classic.

- 2 cups (12 ounces) semisweet chocolate chips
- 1/4 cup (1/2 stick, or 55 g) butter or margarine
- 2 tablespoons (28 ml) canola oil
- 2 cups (100 g) mini marshmallows
- 1/2 cup (83 g) golden raisins
- 1/4 cup (41 g) dried cranberries
- 1 cup (150 g) broken pretzel sticks
- 1/2 cup (55 g) chopped pecans

Butter an 8-inch (20 cm) square cake pan. In a saucepan over medium heat, melt the chocolate with the butter and oil. Set aside to cool for 5 minutes. Stir in the marshmallows, raisins, cranberries, pretzels, and pecans, mixing to combine. Pour into the prepared pan, cover, and refrigerate until firm. Cut into squares and serve.

Prep = 15 minutes **Cook** = 2 hours **Yield** = 36 pieces

White Chocolate Fruit and Nut Bark

Blueberries, cherries, cranberries, and strawberries are all popular dried fruit options now—we've come a long way since the days of California raisins and prunes. A bit more decadent than they are on their own, cranberries, blueberries, and golden raisins are bathed in velvety white chocolate in this bark recipe.

12	ounces (340 g) white chocolate chips or squares, chopped
½	teaspoon orange extract
¼	cup (41 g) chopped golden raisins
¼	cup (41 g) dried blueberries
½	cup (50 g) mini marshmallows
½	cup (83 g) dried cranberries, divided
¾	cup (83 g) coarsely chopped pecans

Melt the chocolate in the top of a double boiler. Add the orange extract, golden raisins, blueberries, marshmallows, ¼ cup of the dried cranberries, and ¼ cup of the pecans. Stir to combine. Line a 9 × 12-inch (22.5 × 30 cm) sheet pan with waxed paper. Spread the mixture evenly over the waxed paper into an 8 x 10-inch (20 × 25 cm) rectangle. Sprinkle the remaining dried cranberries and pecans over the top, pressing them into the chocolate just so they stick. Let stand to cool for about 10 minutes. Cover and refrigerate until hardened, about 2 hours. When ready to serve, cut into bars or simply break into pieces.

Prep = 10 minutes **Cook** =10 minutes **Chill** = 2 hours 10 minutes
Yield = About 2 dozen pieces

Cereal Bark

Breakfast cereals are easy and accessible ingredients that many households have on hand. When coated with chocolate, they make simple (but sweet) snacks for kids who love to help in the kitchen—especially since they can "play" with their food. The two cereals suggested can be replaced with any of your favorites.

12 ounces (340 g) white chocolate chips or squares, chopped (about 1½ cups)

1 cup (115 g) whole-grain wheat and barley cereal (such as Grape-Nuts)

2 cups (37 g) flavored whole wheat O-shaped cereals (such as Cheerios, Banana Nut flavor)

Melt the chocolate in the top of a double boiler. Line a 9 × 12-inch (22.5 × 30 cm) sheet pan with waxed paper. Pour the wheat and barley cereal in an even layer on the waxed paper. Top with the melted chocolate. Pour the o-shaped cereal over the chocolate, pressing into the chocolate to make the cereal stick. Let stand for 10 minutes to cool. Cover with plastic wrap and refrigerate until hardened, at least 2 hours.

To serve, remove bark from pan and break into pieces. Store in an airtight container for up to 5 days.

Prep = 5 minutes **Cook** = 10 minutes **Chill** = 2 hours
Yield = About 2 dozen clusters

Chocolate-Covered Crackle Squares

With chocolate on your mind, you can stroll down the cereals aisle of any grocery store and think of endless ways to use them. A simple starter: melt marshmallows and use them to coat any cereal. My sweet tooth aches for sugar-frosted cornflake cereal. Why not try it even sweeter?

3   tablespoons (42 g) unsalted butter or margarine
1   (10-ounce, 280 g) bag large marshmallows
½   teaspoon pure vanilla extract
3   ounces (85 g) dark chocolate, grated
4   cups (156 g) sugar-frosted cereal flakes
    (such as Kellogg's Frosted Flakes)

Butter the bottom and sides of a 9 × 13 × 2-inch (22.5 × 32.5 × 5 cm) baking dish. In a large stockpot over medium-high heat, melt the butter and add marshmallows, stirring constantly until melted. Remove from heat and add the vanilla and chocolate, stirring until melted and mixed through. Pour in the cereal, stirring to thoroughly coat. Working quickly, scrape mixture into the prepared baking dish, pressing lightly into pan. Allow to cool, and cut into squares to serve.

Prep = 15 minutes   **Cook** = 30 minutes
Yield = 24 squares

Chocolate Rice Cereal Mounds

Chocolate is the perfect match with marshmallow and crisp cereal, right? Of course it is. To make these treats even more fun, there is an added touch of candy-coated chocolates.

4	tablespoons ($\frac{1}{2}$ stick, or 55 g) unsalted butter or margarine
1	(10-ounce, 280 g) bag large marshmallows
3	ounces (85 g) dark chocolate, grated
$6\frac{1}{2}$	cups (182 g) crispy rice cereal
$\frac{1}{2}$	cup (90 g) mini candy-coated chocolates (such as M&M'S)

In a large stockpot over medium-high heat, melt the butter. Add the marshmallows, stirring constantly until melted. Remove from heat and add the chocolate, stirring until melted and mixed through. Pour in the cereal and candies, stirring to coat thoroughly. Working quickly, spoon mounds of the cereal mixture out onto prepared sheet pan. Allow to cool and serve. Alternatively, scrape mixture into a buttered 9 × 13 × 2-inch (22.5 × 32.5 × 5 cm) baking dish, pressing lightly into the pan. Allow to cool and cut into large squares.

Prep = 15 minutes **Chill** = 30 minutes **Yield** = 24 mounds

Chocolate Pecan Turtles

These are just like the turtles found in the candy shop, and best of all, they are easy to make. Using store-bought caramel candies melted with cream is the easiest way to make the caramel layer. Use good-quality chocolate and pecans for best results. If you prefer darker, richer chocolate, use a premium dark chocolate or mix it up and make the bottom out of milk chocolate and the top out of dark.

- 3 cups (18 ounces, or 510 g) semisweet chocolate morsels
- 96 pecan halves (about 2 cups, or 200 g)
- 42 caramels, unwrapped
- 3 tablespoons (45 ml) whipping cream

In the top of a double boiler, melt the chocolate. Drop the chocolate by tablespoonfuls onto waxed paper-lined sheet pans, forming 24 (about 1½-inch, or 3.75 cm) circles. You will not use all of the chocolate; set the remainder aside. Arrange four pecan halves over each chocolate circle. Place in the refrigerator to chill until firm, about 30 minutes. Place caramels and cream in the top of a double boiler and stir until melted and smooth. Spoon caramel mixture over pecans. Reheat reserved chocolate, dropping onto caramel. Refrigerate again until well chilled, about 1 hour. Serve candies.

Prep = 30 minutes **Chill** = 1 hour 30 minutes **Yield** = 24 candies

Nutty Oatmeal Cookie Brownies

Take a classic chocolate brownie and top it with oatmeal cookies? How heavenly!

8   ounces (225 g) dark chocolate, chopped

12 tablespoons (1½ sticks, or 167 g) unsalted butter or margarine, softened

¾   cup (180 g) packed light brown sugar

¾   cup (150 g) granulated sugar

1   teaspoon pure vanilla extract

¼   teaspoon salt

3   eggs

1   cup (120 g) all-purpose flour

½   teaspoon baking powder

1   cup (110 g) chopped pecans, toasted

OATMEAL COOKIE CRUMBLE:

8   tablespoons (1 stick, or 112 g) unsalted butter or margarine, softened

1   cup (80 g) whole oats (not quick cooking)

¼   cup (30 g) all-purpose flour

1   teaspoon ground cinnamon

⅓   cup (75 g) packed light brown sugar

½   teaspoon baking powder

Preheat the oven to 350°F (180°C, or gas mark 4). Prepare an 8-inch (20 cm) square baking dish by spraying with nonstick cooking spray. In the top of a double boiler, melt the chocolate, then set aside. With a stand mixer and paddle, beat the butter with the sugars until and creamy, about 3 minutes. Add the vanilla, salt, and eggs; beat until well combined. Add the melted chocolate, flour, and baking powder. Beat just to combine. Stir in the nuts. Spoon batter into the prepared dish.

Make the topping: In a mixing bowl combine all the ingredients and, using a fork, mash together until a crumbly texture. Layer the oatmeal crumble over the top of the batter, pressing gently into it. Bake on the center rack of oven for 30 to 35 minutes, until a wooden skewer inserted into the center comes out almost clean. Remove from oven and cool for 20 minutes; cut and serve.

Prep = 15 minutes **Cook** = 30 to 35 minutes **Chill** = 20 minutes
Yield = 16 brownies

Chocolate Peanut Butter Pastry Bites

Quick and easy desserts are perfect when you're having guests. These are easy to prepare and quick to be eaten! For added flavor, try chopped pecans and orange zest instead of the candy crumbs, and replace the vanilla with orange extract.

15	mini prepared phyllo dessert cups
4	ounces (115 g) dark chocolate, chopped
2	ounces (55 g) milk chocolate, chopped
2	tablespoons (28 g) unsalted butter
1	tablespoon (15 ml) heavy whipping cream
3	tablespoons (48 g) creamy peanut butter
1/2	teaspoon pure vanilla extract
1/3	cup (50 g) toffee bits (such as Heath)
	Whipped cream, for garnish
	Ground cinnamon, for garnish

Preheat oven to 350°F (180°C, or gas mark 4). Line mini muffin tins with phyllo cups. In the top of a double boiler, melt the chocolates with the butter and the heavy cream, stirring until smooth and combined. Remove from the heat and stir in the peanut butter, vanilla and toffee bits. Let mixture cool for about 20 minutes, until it reaches a thick consistency. Using a pastry bag or a resealable plastic bag with one corner cut off, pipe the mixture into each pastry cup, filling to the top, cover with plastic wrap, and refrigerate until set, at least 30 minutes. When ready to serve, top each with a dollop of whipped cream and a sprinkle of cinnamon.

Prep = 20 minutes **Cook** = 1 hour
Yield = 15 bite size pastries

Chocolate Almond Toffee

This simple recipe yields results that are quite delicious. Store-bought chocolate bars are not only easier to work with but make spreading the chocolate evenly much easier, too. As elsewhere, the nuts can be substituted with any of your favorites: pecans, hazelnuts, or the like.

½	cup (48 g) sliced almonds
14	tablespoons (1 stick plus 6 tablespoons, or 196 g) unsalted butter, plus extra for buttering pan
1	cup (200 g) granulated sugar
2	tablespoons (28 ml) cold water
1	teaspoon pure vanilla extract
	Pinch of salt
6	ounces (170 g) thin chocolate bars (about 4)

Preheat oven to 350°F (180°C, or gas mark 4). Scatter almonds evenly over 10 × 13-inch (25 × 32.5 cm) sheet pan and bake until toasted and fragrant, 5 to 7 minutes. Remove the almonds from oven and transfer them to a bowl. Once cooled, coat the sheet pan generously with butter and set aside.

In a saucepan over medium-high heat, combine butter, sugar, and water. Bring to a boil, stirring constantly with a wooden spoon, about 10 minutes. Remove spoon and continue to cook to brittle stage, 300 to 310°F (150° to 154°C) on a candy thermometer. Remove from heat and stir in almonds, vanilla, and salt. Pour out the mixture onto prepared sheet pan, spreading to ¼-inch (0.6 cm) thickness. Top immediately with chocolate bars, spreading as they melt. Let cool completely and break into pieces. Store in an airtight container.

Prep = 10 minutes **Cook** = 30 minutes **Chill** = 4 hours
Yield = About 3 cups candy

Marcona Almond and White Chocolate Brittle

Though it's more common to find peanuts in brittle, Marcona almonds are too delicious not to use in this crunchy, mouth-watering candy. Dipping it in white chocolate adds a heavenly sweet layer. These candies are great to make ahead of time and pack for gifts or a party. Individual cellophane bags filled with brittle and tied with ribbon make great holiday gifts.

- 1½ cups (300 g) granulated sugar
- ¾ cup (248 g) light corn syrup
- 3 tablespoons (45 ml) water
- 1 teaspoon pure vanilla extract
- 3 tablespoons (42 g) unsalted butter
- 1 teaspoon baking soda
- 1½ cups (218 g) salted Marcona almonds
- 10 ounces (288 g) white chocolate, chopped

In a saucepan over medium-high heat, combine the sugar, corn syrup, water, and vanilla. Stir until the mixture begins to boil. Cover and boil for 3 minutes. Uncover and brush the inside of the pan with a pastry brush dipped in cold water to release any sugar crystals that have formed on the sides. Continue cooking until a candy thermometer registers 280°F (138°C), 12 to 15 minutes.

Remove from the heat and add the butter, stirring until it melts and is incorporated. Return the pan to the heat and cook, stirring occasionally, until a candy thermometer registers 300°F (150°C), 7 to 10 minutes. Working quickly and carefully, remove the pan from the heat and add the baking soda, stirring constantly until incorporated. Stir in the almonds. Pour the brittle onto the prepared cookie sheet, spreading evenly. Let cool, then break into small pieces. Melt the white chocolate in the top of a double boiler and dip individual pieces into it, coating one side. Lay the pieces out on waxed paper to set.

Prep = 10 minutes **Cook** = 30 minutes **Chill** = 2 hours
Yield = About 4 cups of candy

Chocolate Orange Pecan Tassies

I have scented these holiday classics with a refreshing hint of orange and added chocolate.

CHOCOLATE PASTRY:
- 1³/₄ cups (210 g) all-purpose flour
- ¹/₄ cup (23 g) unsweetened cocoa powder
- 1 tablespoon (6 g) confectioners' sugar
- 2 (3-ounce, or 85 g) packages cream cheese, softened
- ²/₃ cup (150 g) unsalted butter, softened

FILLING:
- 3 large eggs
- ³/₄ cup (150 g) granulated sugar
- ³/₄ cup (248 g) light corn syrup
- 1 tablespoon (6 g) orange zest
- 3 tablespoons (45 ml) fresh orange juice
- 3 tablespoons (42 g) butter or margarine, melted
- 1 teaspoon pure vanilla extract
- ³/₄ cup (83 g) finely chopped pecans
- ²/₃ cup (120 g) mini semisweet chocolate chips
- 3 ounces (85 g) dark chocolate, melted, for garnish

For Chocolate Pastry Cups: In a bowl, whisk together the flour, cocoa, and confectioners' sugar. In the bowl of a stand mixer with paddle attachment, beat cream cheese and butter until creamy. Gradually add the cocoa mixture, beating on low to combine. Scrape the dough onto a sheet of waxed paper and form into a disk. Wrap dough with waxed paper, and chill at least 2 hours. Divide dough in half, and then into 24 pieces. Roll pieces into balls, flatten with the palm of your hand, and place them in lightly greased miniature muffin pans, pressing to form cups. Cover and chill until ready to fill and bake.

For the Filling: Whisk the first five ingredients together until blended. Add melted butter, vanilla, pecans, and chocolate chips; stir to combine. Spoon the filling into each of the pastry cups, filling three-quarters. Bake at 325°F (170°C, or gas mark 3) for 25 minutes or until set. Cool for 5 minutes in pans; transfer to wire racks to cool. Drizzle or pipe melted dark chocolate over each tassie in a crisscross pattern.

Prep = 20 minutes **Chill** = 2 hours for dough **Cook** = 25 minutes
Yield = 4 dozen

Johnnie's Hokey Pokey Cookies

My friend Johnnie owned a successful bakery for many years. Compiled in a small pocket notebook (which he carried everywhere) are some of his most popular recipes, a few of which he has generously shared with me. These cookies are one of his favorites.

3½ cups (420 g) all-purpose flour
1 cup (80 g) rolled oats
½ teaspoon salt
1 teaspoon baking powder
1 teaspoon baking soda
1 teaspoon ground cinnamon
2 cups (450 g) packed light brown sugar
1 cup (225 g) shortening
2 eggs
½ teaspoon pure vanilla extract
1 cup (235 ml) water
2 cups (350 g) semisweet chocolate chips
2½ cups (175 g) flaked coconut
1½ cups (248 g) raisins (mix golden and regular if you like)
1½ cups (143 g) sliced almonds

Preheat oven to 375°F (190°C, or gas mark 5). Line two baking sheets with parchment paper or a Silpat. In a mixing bowl, whisk together the flour, oats, salt, baking powder, baking soda, and cinnamon; set aside. With a stand mixer fitted with the paddle, cream the brown sugar and shortening until smooth, about 3 minutes on medium speed. Add the eggs and vanilla and beat to combine. Add the water and the flour mixture, alternating between the two, beginning and ending with the flour mixture; beat until just combined. Remove the bowl from mixer and, by hand, mix in the chocolate chips, coconut, raisins, and almonds. Scoop the dough by heaping tablespoonfuls onto the baking sheets. Bake on the middle rack of the oven for 12 to 15 minutes, just until the cookies begin to brown. Remove, and let cool on sheet pans for 5 minutes. Transfer to cooling racks to cool completely.

Prep = 20 minutes **Cook** = 12 to 15 minutes per batch
Yield = 3 dozen large cookies

Nutty 'Nilla Marshmallow Fudge

Rich, smooth, and velvety, this fudge is chock full of nuts and marshmallows—a real treat to savor.

- 5 tablespoons (70 g) unsalted butter, melted
- 1 cup (225 g) light brown sugar
- 1 cup (200 g) granulated sugar
- 1/4 cup (83 g) light corn syrup
- 3/4 cup (175 ml) heavy whipping cream
- 1 tablespoon (15 ml) pure vanilla extract
- 1/8 teaspoon salt
- 2 ounces (55 g) bittersweet chocolate, chopped
- 3 ounces (85 g) milk chocolate, chopped
- 1/2 cup (60 g) chopped walnuts
- 1/2 cup (55 g) chopped pecans
- 1 3/4 cups (88 g) miniature marshmallows

Butter the sides and bottom of an 8-inch (20 cm) square cake pan. In a large saucepan over medium-high heat, bring the butter, brown sugar, sugar, corn syrup, half-and-half, and vanilla to a boil, stirring for 3 minutes. Add the bittersweet and milk chocolate, stirring constantly, and continue to boil until mixture reaches 234°F (112°C) on a candy thermometer, about 7 to 10 minutes. Remove from heat and let cool to 110°F (43°C), about 15 minutes. Beat until creamy, about 3 minutes. Stir in nuts. Spread marshmallows in an even layer on the bottom of the cake pan, pour fudge mixture over marshmallows, spreading to an even layer. Cover with plastic wrap, pressing the plastic directly on the fudge; refrigerate until chilled, at least 1 hour.

Variations:

Cherry Nut: Replace walnuts and pecans with chopped hazelnuts and use dried cherries instead of miniature marshmallows.

Pistachio Ginger: Replace walnuts and pecans with pistachios. Omit marshmallows and add 1/4 cup minced crystallized ginger with the pistachios.

Prep = 20 minutes   **Chill** = 1 hour
Yield = 36 small pieces

Nutty P'Butter Blondies

With a moist, cakelike consistency, these blondies are packed with flavor and crunch.

- 1 cup (120 g) all-purpose flour
- 1/2 cup (50 g) ground rolled oats (not quick-cooking)
- 1 teaspoon baking powder
- 1/4 teaspoon baking soda
- 1/2 teaspoon ground cinnamon
- Pinch of nutmeg
- 1/4 teaspoon salt
- 3/4 cup (195 g) crunchy peanut butter
- 6 tablespoons (83 g) unsalted butter, softened
- 3/4 cup (150 g) granulated sugar
- 3/4 cup (169 g) packed light brown sugar
- 3 large eggs
- 1/2 teaspoon pure vanilla extract
- 1 cup (144 g) coarsely chopped salted peanuts
- 1/2 cup (35 g) flaked coconut
- 6 ounces (170 g) mini semisweet chocolate chips

Preheat oven to 350°F (180°C, or gas mark 4). Spray a 9-inch (22.5 cm) square baking pan with nonstick cooking spray. In a large mixing bowl, whisk the flour, ground oats, baking powder, baking soda, cinnamon, nutmeg, and salt. With a stand mixer and paddle, beat the peanut butter and butter until smooth. Add the sugars beating until creamy, about 2 minutes. Add the eggs one at a time, beating thoroughly after each. Scrape the sides of the bowl with a rubber spatula and beat in the vanilla. Add the dry ingredients, beating on low speed just to incorporate. Remove from the mixer, cleaning the paddle sides of the bowl. Stir in the peanuts, coconut, and chocolate chips. Scrape the dough into the baking pan. Place on the middle rack of the oven and bake for 45 to 50 minutes, until the top is toasted and a skewer inserted into the center comes out relatively clean. Transfer to a cooling rack and cool for 1 hour. Gently invert onto a cooling rack to allow to cool completely. Cut into bars or squares and serve.

Prep = 20 minutes **Cook** = 45 to 50 minutes **Chill** = 1 hour
Yield = 16 squares or bars

Oatmeal-Cherry-Chocolate Cookies

These oatmeal cookies are turned up a notch with tart dried cherries and coconut. Banana adds flavor and a nutritional boost that suits the chocolate chips well.

$1^{1}/_{2}$ cups (180 g) all-purpose flour
$^{1}/_{2}$ cup (35 g) flaked coconut
$^{3}/_{4}$ cup (60 g) rolled oats (not quick-cooking)
$1^{1}/_{2}$ teaspoons baking soda
$^{1}/_{2}$ teaspoon salt
  1   teaspoon ground cinnamon
  1   cup (225 g) packed light brown sugar
  8   tablespoons (1 stick, or 112 g) unsalted butter, softened
$^{1}/_{2}$ teaspoon pure vanilla extract
  1   very ripe banana, mashed (about $^{1}/_{2}$ cup, or 113 g)
  2   eggs, at room temperature
$^{1}/_{2}$ cup (83 g) dried cherries, chopped
$^{1}/_{2}$ cup (60 g) chopped walnuts
$^{3}/_{4}$ cup (131 g) milk chocolate chips

Preheat oven to 325°F (170°C, or gas mark 3). Line baking sheet with parchment paper or a Silpat. In a mixing bowl, combine the flour with the coconut, oats, baking soda, salt, and cinnamon. In the bowl of a stand mixer, fitted with the paddle attachment, beat the sugar with the butter until smooth and creamy, about 3 minutes. Add the vanilla, banana, and eggs and blend just to combine. Add the flour mixture, one-third at a time, blending just to combine after each addition. Remove bowl from mixer and blend in, by hand, the cherries, walnuts, and chocolate chips. Drop the dough in heaping tablespoons about 2 inches apart on the baking sheet. Bake on middle rack of oven for 12 to 15 minutes. Remove, let cool for 5 minutes, transfer to cooling rack, and let cool completely.

Prep = 15 minutes   **Cook** = 12 to 15 minutes   **Chill** = 20 minutes
Yield = 2 dozen cookies

Heavenly White Chocolate Chip Cookies

Rich and buttery with a hint of orange, these cookies are a sure hit for any bake sale or afternoon treat. For an even more heavenly experience, dip each cookie halfway into melted white chocolate.

- 1 cup (2 sticks, 225 g) unsalted butter, softened
- 4 tablespoons (½ stick, or 55 g) margarine, softened
- 1 cup (225 g) packed light brown sugar
- 1 cup (200 g) granulated sugar
- ½ teaspoon orange extract
- ½ teaspoon butter flavoring (optional)
- 1 teaspoon pure vanilla extract
- 2 large eggs
- 4 cups (440 g) pastry flour
- 1½ teaspoons baking soda
- 2 cups (220 g) chopped pecans
- 2 cups (350 g) white chocolate chips

Preheat oven to 375°F (190°C, or gas mark 5). Line baking sheets with parchment paper or a Silpat. In the bowl of a stand mixer fitted with the paddle attachment, cream the butter and margarine with the sugars until creamy and smooth, about 3 minutes. Add the orange extract, butter flavor, vanilla, and eggs; beat until just combined. Add half the flour and baking soda; blend on low just to combine. Add the remaining flour and baking soda; blend on low just to combine. Remove the bowl from mixer and stir in the pecans and white chocolate chips by hand. Drop heaping tablespoons of dough onto prepared baking sheets. Bake on the center rack of oven for 12 to 14 minutes. Remove, let cool on baking pan for 5 minutes, and transfer to a rack to cool completely.

Prep = 20 minutes **Cook** = 12 to 14 minutes (in batches)
Yield = 4 dozen large cookies

Chocolate Pecan Pralines

Pecan pralines are a classic Southern dessert that are featured prominently in all of my mother's dessert spreads. Added chocolate takes them from delightful to decadent. Covered, these will keep for about five days.

2½   cups (250 g) whole pecans
1¼   cups (295 ml) buttermilk
1¼   teaspoons baking soda
3½   cups (700 g) granulated sugar
3   tablespoons (60 g) light corn syrup
4   ounces (115 g) premium dark chocolate, grated
5   tablespoons (70 g) unsalted butter
2½   tablespoons (38 ml) vanilla extract
1   tablespoon (15 ml) dark rum

Preheat the oven to 350°F (180°C, or gas mark 4). Scatter the pecans across a sheet pan in an even layer. Toast in the oven for about 7 minutes, until browned and fragrant. Remove and set aside. In a large saucepan over medium heat combine the buttermilk, baking soda, sugar, corn syrup, chocolate, and butter. Cook, stirring occasionally, until the mixture reaches the soft-ball stage, between 234° and 240°F (112° and 116°C) on a candy thermometer, about 20 minutes. Remove from heat, and add the vanilla, rum, and pecans. Beat the candy with a wooden spoon until it becomes opaque and creamy, about 10 minutes. Drop the candy by tablespoonfuls onto oiled waxed paper. Let cool thoroughly, then wrap individually in plastic wrap. Store at room temperature for about 5 days.

Prep = 20 minutes **Chill** = 2 hours
Yield = About 24 pieces

Snow-Capped Canyon Cookies

Crinkle, Crackle, or Lace—whichever name they go by, these cookies are a staple in chocolate baking. By rolling dough balls in powdered sugar, snow-capped crevasses bake right into these delightfully flavorful treats.

  6   ounces (170 g) bittersweet chocolate chips or squares, chopped
1¹/₂ cups (180 g) all-purpose flour
 ¹/₂ cup (45 g) unsweetened cocoa powder
 ¹/₂ teaspoon ground nutmeg
 ¹/₄ teaspoon salt
  2   tablespoons (1 stick, 112 g) unsalted butter, softened
  1   cup (225 g) packed light brown sugar
1¹/₂ cups (300 g) granulated sugar, divided
  2   large eggs
  1   teaspoon pure vanilla extract
 ¹/₂ cup (120 ml) whole milk
  1   cup (100 g) confectioners' sugar

Melt chocolate in the top of a double boiler and set aside to cool. In a large mixing bowl, whisk together the flour, cocoa powder, salt, and nutmeg; set aside. In the bowl of a stand mixer fitted with the paddle attachment, beat the butter with the brown sugar and ¹/₂ cup (100 g) of the granulated sugar until creamy and smooth, about 3 minutes. Mix in the eggs and the vanilla. Add the melted chocolate, beating well to combine. Scrape down sides of bowl and add half the flour mixture, beating on low to combine. Mix in the milk, followed by the remaining flour mixture, beating just to incorporate. Divide the dough into three equal pieces, form pieces into disks, wrap in plastic wrap, and refrigerate for at least 2 hours.

Preheat oven to 350°F (180°C, or gas mark 4). Line baking sheets with parchment paper or Silpats. Divide each piece of dough into 1-inch (2.5 cm) balls. Roll each in granulated sugar and then in confectioners' sugar. Place the balls on sheet pans 2 inches (5 cm) apart. Bake until cracks form over the tops, about 14 minutes. Transfer to cooling racks to cool.

Prep = 20 minutes **Chill** = 2 hours **Cook** = 14 minute
Yield = 5 dozen cookies

Chocolate Date-Nut Logs

Every holiday season in my mother's house has included these luxurious sliced sweets. I have added chocolate and cocoa nibs for a modern approach, lending a lively crunch. Other dried fruits such as cranberries or cherries are an option, too; they will add a light tartness to the logs.

1	(8-ounce, 225 g) package chopped dates
1	cup (200 g) granulated sugar
8	tablespoons (1 stick, or 112 g) butter
1	teaspoon vanilla extract
1	egg
2	cups (56 g) crisp rice cereal
2	cups (220 g) chopped pecans
1/3	cup (58 g) semisweet chocolate chips
1/2	cup (55 g) cocoa nibs
1	cup (70 g) flaked coconut, toasted

Combine first five ingredients in a large saucepan; cook over low heat for 10 minutes, stirring constantly. Remove mixture from the heat; add rice cereal, pecans, chocolate chips, and cocoa nibs; stir well. Scrape mixture out onto a waxed paper-lined surface and, using hands, shape into two 11-inch (27.5 cm) logs. Roll each in toasted coconut, pressing lightly so it sticks to logs. Wrap each log separately in plastic wrap and refrigerate for at least 2 hours. When ready to serve, remove from refrigerator, unwrap, and slice thinly.

To toast coconut: Preheat oven to 350°F (180°C, or gas mark 4). Spread an even layer over an ungreased sheet pan. Place on the center rack of oven and bake for 10 minutes, or until coconut begins to turn tan in color.

Prep = 10 minutes **Cook** = 10 minutes **Chill** = 2 hours
Yield = About 24 slices

Chocolate-Caramel Popcorn

Take movie night to a new level with Chocolate-Caramel Popcorn. This truly indulgent treat is great for children and adults alike. For best results use freshly popped popcorn. If you'd prefer not to mix pecans with peanuts, feel free to use all peanuts or substitute almonds.

 10 cups (80 g) popped popcorn
 1 cup (146 g) dry-roasted peanuts
 ³/₄ cup (83 g) coarsely chopped pecans
 1 cup (225 g) packed light brown sugar
 8 tablespoons (1 stick or, or 112 g) butter or margarine
 ¹/₄ cup (83 g) light corn syrup
 ¹/₄ cup (60 ml) milk
 ³/₄ cup (130 g) semisweet chocolate chips
 ¹/₂ teaspoon baking soda
 ¹/₂ teaspoon pure vanilla extract

Preheat oven to 325°F (170°C, or gas mark 3). Remove any unpopped kernels from the popcorn and discard. Spread the popcorn out on a large baking pan (two if necessary) and top with nuts, spreading evenly. In a saucepan, combine the brown sugar, butter, corn syrup, and milk. Bring to a boil over medium-high heat. Cook without stirring for 5 minutes, remove from the heat, and stir in chocolate until melted. Stir in the baking soda and vanilla. Pour the chocolate mixture over the popcorn, stirring to coat evenly. Bake uncovered for 15 minutes. Stir around once and bake for an additional 5 to 10 minutes, until the mixture is crisp. Let cool, transfer to a large bowl, and serve.

Prep = 20 minutes **Cook** = 20 to 25 minutes
Yield = About 11 cups

White Chocolate-Cranberry Blondies

Blondies can take on a multitude of ingredients—the tartness of cranberries is paired with the crunch of macadamia nuts, resulting in a chewy delight.

- 1 cup (125 g) all-purpose flour
- 1/2 cup (100 g) granulated sugar
- 1/2 teaspoon salt
- 1 teaspoon baking powder
- 1 teaspoon ground cinnamon
- 8 tablespoons (1 stick, or 112 g) unsalted butter or margarine
- 1/2 cup (113 g) light brown sugar
- 1 teaspoon pure vanilla extract
- 2 large eggs
- 1 cup (80 g) rolled oats (not quick-cooking)
- 2/3 cup (110 g) dried cranberries
- 1/2 cup (67 g) chopped macadamia nuts
- 1/2 cup (88 g) white chocolate chips

Preheat oven to 350°F (180°C, or gas mark 4). Spray an 8-inch (20 cm) square baking pan with nonstick cooking spray. Cut two sheets of parchment into rectangles to cover the bottom and come up the sides of the pan with about 2 inches (5 cm) of overhang on each side. Spray with nonstick cooking spray between the sheets and on top.

In a mixing bowl, whisk the flour, granulated sugar, salt, baking powder, and cinnamon. With a stand mixer and paddle beat the butter and brown sugar until fluffy, about 3 minutes. Add the vanilla and the eggs, one at a time, scraping the bowl and beating just until combined after each addition. With the mixer on low, gradually add in the flour mixture, beating just until combined. Mix in 3/4 cup (60 g) of oats, 1/3 cup (55 g) of the cranberries, and all of the macadamia nuts. Pour batter into prepared pan and spread evenly. Sprinkle the batter evenly with remaining oats, cranberries, and white chocolate chips, pressing gently to adhere. Bake on middle rack of oven for 30 minutes, until a wooden skewer inserted in the center comes out clean. Let cool in pan for 30 minutes. Transfer to wire rack to cool completely. Cut into 16 squares and serve.

Prep = 15 minutes **Cook** = 30 minutes **Chill** = 1 hour
Yield = 16 squares

Monster Cookies

Packed with chocolate, nuts, peanut butter, and candy, these cookies are a hit with everyone who tries them. My friend Johnnie shared this recipe with me from his popular library of bakeshop goodies.

- 1 cup (225 g) packed light brown sugar
- 1 cup (200 g) granulated sugar
- 1 cup (225 g) shortening
- 3 large eggs
- 1 teaspoon pure vanilla extract
- 1/2 teaspoon baking soda
- 1 cup (260 g) creamy peanut butter
- 3 cups (240 g) rolled oats
- 1 tablespoon (20 g) light corn syrup
- 1/2 cup (88 g) semisweet chocolate chips
- 1 cup (175 g) candy-coated chocolate candies (such as M&M'S)

Preheat oven to 375°F (190°C, or gas mark 5). Line two baking sheets with parchment or Silpats. In the bowl of a stand mixer fitted with the paddle attachment, blend the sugars and shortening until creamy and smooth, about 3 minutes. Add the eggs and vanilla and blend just until combined. Add the peanut butter, oats, and corn syrup and blend just to combine. Remove bowl and, by hand, stir in the chocolate chips and candy-coated chocolates. Scoop heaping tablespoons of dough 2 inches (5 cm) apart onto the prepared baking sheets. Bake on the center rack of oven for 12 to 15 minutes. Remove cookies from oven and let cool on sheet pans for 5 minutes, then transfer to cooling racks.

Prep = 20 minutes **Cook** = 12 to 15 minutes (in batches)
Yield = 3 dozen large cookies

2

Chocolate Beginnings and Breakfast Greats

Chocolate Chip–Oatmeal Pancakes

Weekend mornings, I am confounded by choice: make a quick breakfast of oatmeal and berries or indulge in pancakes. With this recipe, you can have both.

1½ cups (180 g) all-purpose flour, sifted
½ cup (60 g) whole wheat flour
3 tablespoons (38 g) granulated sugar
2 teaspoons baking powder
1 teaspoon baking soda
1½ teaspoons ground cinnamon
1 teaspoon salt
2 eggs, lightly beaten
2¼ cups (530 ml) buttermilk
4 tablespoons (½ stick, or 55 g) unsalted butter, melted
½ teaspoon vanilla extract
1 cup (235 g) cooked rolled oats
½ cup (88 g) semisweet chocolate chips
½ cup (55 g) cocoa nibs (optional)
Butter and vegetable oil, for cooking
Softened butter, for serving
Warm maple syrup, for serving

In a large mixing bowl, whisk together the flour, wheat flour, sugar, baking powder, baking soda, cinnamon, and salt. In a separate small bowl, beat the eggs with the buttermilk to combine. Pour the buttermilk mixture into the dry ingredients, add the melted butter, and, using a whisk, stir to combine. Add the vanilla, oatmeal, chocolate chips, and cocoa nibs, stirring just to combine. Working in batches, melt 1 tablespoon (14 g) butter with 1 tablespoon (15 ml) vegetable oil in a large nonstick pan over medium heat. Pour ½ cup (120 ml) portions of batter into the pan to make pancakes. Cook for 4 minutes; when pockets of air form all over, flip and cook for an additional 3 minutes, until cooked through. Continue cooking all the pancakes, adding butter and oil to the pan as necessary. When using butter, it may be necessary to wipe the pan down a couple of times between batches as the butterfat begins to burn in the pan. Serve pancakes warm with butter and maple syrup.

Prep = 15 minutes **Cook** = 20 minutes
Yield = 4 servings (about 16 pancakes)

Chocolate Chip Granola

If you can't find dried strawberries, substitute dried cranberries or cherries, or just omit completely.

 2 cups (160 g) (not quick-cooking) rolled oats
 1/2 cup (58 g) wheat germ
 1/4 cup (28 g) coarsely chopped pecans
 1/4 cup (24 g) sliced almonds
 1/4 cup (30 g) white sesame seeds
 1/4 cup (18 g) shredded sweetened coconut
 1/4 cup (36 g) raw sunflower seeds
 1/2 cup (88 g) semisweet chocolate chips
 1/4 cup (28 g) cocoa nibs
 1/2 cup (35 g) dried strawberries
 2 tablespoons (38 ml) canola oil
 3 tablespoons (60 ml) honey
 1 tablespoon (6 g) unsweetened cocoa powder
 1 teaspoon ground cinnamon
 1 teaspoon pure vanilla extract
   Milk, for serving
   Sliced fresh fruit such as nectarines, peaches, bananas, pears, plums, mangoes, or berries, for serving (optional)

Preheat oven broiler. In a large mixing bowl, combine the oats, wheat germ, pecans, almonds, sesame seeds, coconut, and sunflower seeds. Spread mixture on a baking sheet in an even layer and bake under the broiler, watching very carefully, stirring and turning every 30 to 45 seconds, cooking until all is browned evenly. Remove from oven and set aside to cool. In a saucepan heat the oil, honey, cocoa powder, cinnamon and vanilla until just bubbling, stirring to combine. Remove from the heat and let cool for 10 minutes. Transfer the dry granola mixture to the mixing bowl and stir in the chocolate chips, cocoa nibs and dried strawberries. Pour half the honey mixture over the dry mixture, stirring to evenly coat. Pour a bit more honey mixture into granola just until the granola forms little clusters. Too much honey mixture will make it soupy. Spread out granola mixture onto sheet pan and allow to cool and harden. Serve with milk as a cereal or mixed with yogurt or trifle. Granola can be kept in an airtight container for up to 1 week.

Prep = 30 minutes **Yield** = About 5 cups

Sweet S'Mores French Toast

There is a great pastry shop in downtown Providence, Café Choklad, where I frequently get coffee. One of their signature dishes is the S'Mores Panini. My question: Why wait for lunch to enjoy something so divine?

- 4 eggs
- 2 tablespoons (30 g) light brown sugar
- 1 cup (235 ml) milk
- ¼ cup (60 ml) heavy cream
- Pinch of salt
- 1 loaf sweet brioche or challah bread, sliced into twelve 1-inch (2.5 cm) thick slices
- 6 ounces (170 g) semisweet chocolate chips, melted
- 2 cups (385 g) marshmallow creme
- Butter, for cooking
- 1½ cups (180 g) graham cracker crumbs
- Confectioners' sugar, for dusting

Preheat oven to 250°F (120°C, or gas mark ½), to keep french toast warm during cooking.

In a mixing bowl, whisk the eggs with the brown sugar until smooth. Add the milk, heavy cream, and salt, whisk to combine well, and set aside.

Working with two slices of bread at a time, lay them on a clean, dry surface. Spread chocolate on one slice and marshmallow creme on the other. With the chocolate and creme on the inside, press the two slices of bread together. Repeat process with remaining ten slices of bread.

Working with two French toast at a time, heat 1 tablespoon (14 g) butter in a large skillet over low to medium heat. Drench two toasts in egg batter, then dredge each side in graham-cracker crumbs and place in skillet, cooking on one side until browned, about 3 minutes. Turn and brown the other side for about 2 minutes. Transfer toasts to plate, keeping warm. Repeat, cooking all french toasts, adding butter to pan as needed.

Slice each sandwich in half. Divide the french toasts among six warmed plates and serve dusted with confectioners' sugar.

Prep = 10 minutes   **Cook** = 20 minutes   **Yield** = 6 servings

Chocolate Banana Quick Bread

Banana bread is a classic that packs a lot of flavor. Adding chocolate makes something good even better. Enjoy it toasted with cherry jam or chocolate-hazelnut spread.

- 2 cups (240 g) all-purpose flour
- 1 teaspoon baking soda
- 1 teaspoon baking powder
- 1 teaspoon ground nutmeg
- ½ teaspoon ground ginger
- ½ teaspoon salt
- ½ cup (120 ml) chocolate milk
- 5 ounces (140 g) bittersweet chocolate, chopped
- 6 tablespoons (83 g) unsalted butter or margarine, softened
- ¾ cup (150 g) granulated sugar
- 1 cup (225 g) very ripe mashed bananas (about 2 bananas)
- 3 eggs, lightly beaten
- ⅓ cup (80 g) sour cream
- ¾ cup (90 g) chopped walnuts
- ½ cup (88 g) semisweet chocolate chips

Preheat oven to 350°F (180°C, or gas mark 4). Butter and flour a 9 x 5-inch (22.5 x 13 cm) loaf pan. In a mixing bowl, whisk the flour, baking soda, baking powder, nutmeg, and salt; set aside. In a small saucepan, heat the chocolate milk just until steaming and bubbles form around the edge. Remove from heat, stir in the 5 ounces (140 g) of chocolate, stir until melted; set aside. In the bowl of a stand mixer fitted with the paddle attachment, beat the butter and sugar until smooth, about 3 minutes. Add the banana and 1 egg, beat to combine. Add remaining eggs one at a time, beating after each addition. Add the sour cream and blend. Add one-third of the flour mixture and blend. Add the chocolate milk mixture and blend. Add remaining flour mixture, blending just to combine. Remove bowl. Scrape the sides, and stir in the walnuts and chocolate chips by hand. Pour the batter into the prepared loaf pan and bake until the bread is golden and dry, about 70 to 80 minutes—the sides will pull away from the pan, a skewer inserted in the middle will come out clean. Remove from the oven and let cool for 20 minutes in the pan. Remove from pan and let cool completely before slicing to serve.

Prep = 20 minutes **Cook** = 70 to 80 minutes
Chill = 60 to 80 minutes **Yield** = 1 loaf (about 16 slices)

Power Breakfast Muffins

These are powered up with nutrients to help jump-start your day. Packed with flavor and texture, these muffins will fuel you.

1 cup (120 g) all-purpose flour
1 cup (125 g) whole wheat flour
¾ cup (75 g) oat bran
¼ cup (23 g) unsweetened cocoa powder
½ cup (115 g) packed dark brown sugar
1½ cups (120 g) rolled oats (not quick-cooking)
1½ teaspoons baking powder
1½ teaspoons baking soda
1½ teaspoons ground cinnamon
1 teaspoon ground ginger
¼ teaspoon salt
3 eggs
½ cup (120 ml) canola oil
½ cup (123 g) unsweetened applesauce
½ cup (115 g) light sour cream
1½ cups (180 g) peeled and grated carrots
½ cup (83 g) dried cranberries
½ cup (83 g) golden raisins
1 cup (175 g) semisweet chocolate chips
½ cup (73 g) unsalted sunflower seeds
½ cup (65 g) slivered almonds

Preheat oven to 400°F (200°C, or gas mark 6). Spray sixteen muffin cups with nonstick cooking spray or line with muffin cups.

In a large mixing bowl, combine the flours with the oat bran, cocoa powder, brown sugar, oats, baking powder, baking soda, cinnamon, ginger, and salt. Whisk to combine. In a medium mixing bowl, whisk the eggs with the oil, apple sauce, and sour cream. Pour the wet ingredients into the dry ingredients and stir just to combine. Add the carrots, cranberries, raisins, chocolate chips, sunflower seeds, and almonds, stirring to incorporate. Fill muffin cups to the top with batter. Bake on center rack of oven for 20 to 25 minutes, until browned and firm. Remove and let cool in tins for 10 minutes, then transfer to cooling rack. Eat warm or cool completely before packing to store, refrigerated, for up to 3 days.

Cook = 20 to 25 minutes **Yield** = 16 muffins

Sour Cream Double-Chocolate Muffins

When at bakeries, I am always drawn to their massive chocolaty-chocolate muffins. I created these in honor of those nearly indecent breakfast treats.

- 5 ounces (140 g) unsweetened chocolate
- 8 tablespoons (1 stick, or 112 g) unsalted butter, at room temperature
- 1¼ cups (150 g) all-purpose flour
- ½ cup (45 g) plus ¼ cup (23 g) unsweetened cocoa powder
- ½ cup (40 g) ground oatmeal crumbs
- 2 teaspoons baking powder
- 1 teaspoon baking soda
- ½ teaspoon salt
- 2 extra-large eggs
- 2 teaspoons pure vanilla extract
- 1 cup (230 g) sour cream
- ½ cup (100 g) granulated sugar
- ½ cup (115 g) light brown sugar
- 1½ cups (263 g) semisweet chocolate chips
- ½ cup (50 g) confectioners' sugar, optional

Preheat oven to 375°F (190°C, or gas mark 5). Line the cups of a regular-size muffin pan with muffin cups, or spray with nonstick cooking spray. Place the muffin pan on a slightly larger baking sheet.

In the top of a double boiler, melt the chocolate and butter; set aside. In a large mixing bowl, whisk the flour, ½ cup of cocoa, oatmeal crumbs, baking powder, baking soda, and salt. In another mixing bowl, whisk the eggs, vanilla, sour cream, and sugars. To the flour mixture add the egg and chocolate mixtures, stirring just to combine. Stir in 1 cup of the chocolate chips. Divide the batter evenly among the muffin cups, filling just to the tops. Top each with remaining ½ cup of chocolate chips. (Alternatively, whisk the confectioners' sugar and cocoa. Spoon heaping tablespoons of sugar mixture over each muffin. Bake on center rack of oven for about 30 minutes. Remove from oven and let cool for 5 minutes. Remove muffins from pan and serve.

Prep = 20 minutes **Cook** = 30 minutes **Chill** = 5 minutes
Yield = 1 dozen regular-size muffins or 6 large muffins

Chocolate Blueberry Turnovers

Premade packaged puff pastry is a great way to streamline making pastries. Use them in this indulgent turnover recipe.

1½	cups (218 g) fresh blueberries
2	tablespoons (30 g) lightly packed light brown sugar
1½	tablespoons (11 g) all-purpose flour
1	teaspoon grated orange zest
1½	teaspoons orange juice
½	teaspoon almond extract (or substitute orange or pure vanilla extract)
1	tablespoon (10 g) minced crystallized ginger
	Pinch of salt
1	large egg
2	teaspoons water
2	sheets prepared puff pastry
2	tablespoons (30 g) sanding sugar (coarse decorating sugar)
⅓	cup (32 g) sliced almonds
3	ounces (85 g) dark chocolate, melted (for garnish)

In a mixing bowl, combine first eight ingredients, stirring to combine. Whisk the egg with the water in a small bowl; set aside. Dust a dry, flat work surface with flour. Lay out one puff pastry sheet and roll to an 11 × 16-inch (27.5 × 40 cm) rectangle; cut into six equal squares. Using a pastry brush, brush each edge of the square with the egg wash. Spoon a little less than ¼ cup (65 g) blueberry mixture into the center of each square. Fold one corner to the opposite corner, making a triangle; press the edges together gently with your fingers. Using the tines of a fork, gently press the pastry all around the edge, without piercing the pastry with the fork. Using a thin spatula or bench scraper, transfer each triangle gently to a parchment or Silpat-lined baking sheet. Brush the tops and sides of each pastry with more egg wash and then sprinkle lightly with sanding sugar and sliced almonds. Repeat process with remaining ingredients.

Place on center rack of oven, baking in two batches if necessary. Bake for 20 to 25 minutes, until pastry is golden brown. Remove, let cool for 5 minutes, and serve. Pipe melted chocolate over turnovers.

Prep = 15 minutes **Cook** = 20 to 25 minutes **Yield** = 12 turnovers

Chocolate Pecan Coffee Cake

Even if you can't quite embrace chocolate as a part of your daily breakfast, at least accept it as a special weekend morning treat. This is an easy recipe for a delicious coffee cake that is good well beyond breakfast, too. For added chocolate, drizzle the baked cake with Chocolate Glaze from page 222.

2 1/2   cups (320 g) biscuit mix
1/2   cup (45 g) unsweetened cocoa powder
3/4   cup (150 g) granulated sugar
1/2   cup (120 ml) whole milk
4   tablespoons (1/4 cup, or 55 g) unsalted butter or margarine, melted
1   (8-ounce, or 225 g) package cream cheese, softened
2   ounces (55 g) dark chocolate, melted
1/2   teaspoon pure vanilla extract
2   large eggs
1   cup (110 g) chopped pecans
1/2   cup (88 g) semisweet chocolate chips

Preheat oven to 350°F (180°C, or gas mark 4). In a mixing bowl whisk together the biscuit mix and cocoa powder until combined. Add the 1/4 cup (50 g) sugar, milk, and butter, stirring until well blended. Turn out the dough onto a lightly floured work surface and knead five to six times, until smooth. Press the dough into the bottom and up the sides of an ungreased 9-inch (22.5 cm) round cake pan. In the bowl of a stand mixer fitted with the paddle attachment, combine the cream cheese, melted chocolate, 1/2 cup (100 g) remaining sugar, vanilla, and eggs, beating until smooth and creamy, about 3 minutes. Pour the mixture over the dough; sprinkle with pecans and chocolate chips. Bake for 35 to 40 minutes, until the center is set. Remove and let cool in the pan for 15 minutes. Serve warm.

Prep = 20 minutes   **Cook** = 35 to 40 minutes   **Yield** = 8 servings

Apple-Chocolate Skillet Breakfast Cake

This recipe is similar to an upside-down cake in that you invert the cake from a skillet, then glaze it. Cover and keep this coffee cake refrigerated for up to five days for a breakfast treat that lasts all week.

2	tablespoons (28 g) unsalted butter or margarine, softened plus 8 tablespoons (1 stick, or 112 g)
1	tablespoon (15 ml) vegetable oil
3	tart cooking apples, such as Granny Smith or Braeburn, peeled, cored, and sliced thinly
1 1/2	teaspoons ground cinnamon
1	tablespoon (15 g) granulated sugar, plus 1 1/2 cups (300 g)
1 3/4	cups (210 g) all-purpose flour
1 1/2	teaspoons baking powder
1/4	teaspoon salt
1/4	teaspoon ground nutmeg
1/3	cup (75 g) firmly packed light brown sugar
8	ounces (225 g) cream cheese, softened
2	eggs
1	teaspoon vanilla extract
2	tablespoons (28 ml) fresh orange juice
1/2	cup (123 g) unsweetened applesauce
1/2	cup (88 g) semisweet chocolate chips

COCOA GLAZE:

3/4	cup (75 g) confectioners' sugar, sifted
1/4	cup (23 g) unsweetened cocoa powder, sifted
2	tablespoons (28 ml) condensed skim milk, warmed, plus more as needed
1/2	teaspoon pure vanilla extract
1/2	teaspoon orange extract

Preheat oven to 350°F (180°C, or gas mark 4). Place a 10-inch (25 cm) cast-iron skillet over medium heat. Melt 1 tablespoon (14 g) butter with the vegetable oil, add the apples, and sauté until just turning tender, about 3 minutes. Sprinkle with ½ teaspoon ground cinnamon and 1 tablespoon (15 g) granulated sugar, continue to cook until browned but still a bit firm, about 3 additional minutes. Remove from heat and transfer apples to a plate. Add another 1 tablespoon (14 g) butter to skillet and melt, brushing butter around sides of skillet to coat. Working from the outside of the skillet in, place apple slices one at a time, overlapping each other, creating rings of apples around bottom of pan. Set aside.

In a bowl, whisk together the flour, baking powder, salt, remaining 1 teaspoon cinnamon, and nutmeg. In the bowl of a stand mixer fitted with the paddle attachment, beat together the brown sugar, remaining 1 ½ cups (300 g) sugar, 8 tablespoons (1 stick, or 112 g) butter, and cream cheese until smooth, about 3 minutes. Add the eggs one at a time, beating to combine after each addition. Add the vanilla, orange juice, and applesauce, beating to combine. Add half the flour mixture, beating on low just to combine. Scrape the sides of the bowl and the paddle, add the remaining flour mixture, and beat just to combine. Remove from mixer and stir in, by hand, the chocolate chips. Pour the batter into the skillet, spreading over the apples, being careful not to upset the design. Bake for 60 minutes or until a skewer inserted into the center comes out clean; the top will be golden brown. Transfer to wire rack to cool for 5 minutes. Place a serving plate upside down on top of the skillet, then carefully invert the cake out of the skillet and onto the plate, scraping all of the goodies off of the bottom of the skillet and onto the cake.

Make the glaze: In a small saucepan over medium heat, combine and stir the confectioners' sugar, cocoa, condensed milk, and extracts until melted and smooth. Drizzle cocoa glaze over individual servings of the cake.

Prep = 20 minutes **Cook** = 60 minutes **Yield** = 10 servings

Chocolate Pecan Sticky Buns

A breakfast staple in my childhood home, chocolate sticky buns are a special treat. This simple sweet dough recipe does take time to rise, but its tender, result is worth the wait.

4½	cups (540 g) all-purpose flour
1	envelope (7 g) active dry yeast
1	cup (235 ml) milk
⅓	cup (67 g) sugar
⅓	cup (75 g) butter
½	teaspoon salt
2	eggs

CHOCOLATE SAUCE:

12	ounces (340 g) unsweetened chocolate
8	tablespoons (1 stick, or 112 g) butter
½	cup (120 ml) heavy cream
2	teaspoons pure vanilla extract

FILLING:

3	tablespoons (42 g) unsalted butter
¼	cup (50 g) sugar
3	tablespoons (45 g) packed light brown sugar
1	teaspoon ground cinnamon
¾	cup (83 g) chopped pecans

GLAZE:

1	cup (225 g) packed light brown sugar
8	tablespoons (1 stick, or 112 g) unsalted butter, cut into 4 pieces
¼	cup (83 g) light corn syrup
1½	cups (150 g) pecans (whole pieces)

(Continued on page 76)

(Continued from page 74)

In the mixing bowl of a stand mixer fitted with the paddle attachment, combine 2 cups (240 g) of the flour and the yeast. In a heavy saucepan, combine the milk, sugar, and ⅓ cup (75 g) butter, and salt. Place over medium-high heat and warm until the butter is almost melted, stirring constantly. Add the warmed milk mixture to the flour mixture with eggs and beat on low speed just until combined. Add 1 cup (120 g) more flour; scrape sides of bowl and beater, beat on low speed just to incorporate flour. Increase speed to high and beat for 3 minutes. Add an additional 1 cup (120 g) flour and continue beating. Using remaining flour, dust a work surface. Turn out the dough onto the floured surface and knead to incorporate flour until dough is moderately stiff, smooth, and elastic, 6 to 8 minutes. Place in a lightly oiled bowl; turn once to coat surface. Cover and place in a warm place; let rise until doubled in size, about 1 hour. Punch down the dough, turn out onto a work surface, and divide in half. Cover each half and let rest for 10 minutes.

Meanwhile, prepare the Chocolate Sauce and Filling. In the top of a double boiler, melt the chocolate with the butter and heavy cream. Once melted, remove from heat and stir in vanilla; set aside. For the Filling, in a small saucepan over medium heat, melt the butter. In a mixing bowl, combine the sugar, brown sugar, cinnamon, and pecans. Pour the butter over the dry ingredients. Using a fork, stir just to combine to a crumbly texture.

Preheat oven to 375°F (190°C, or gas mark 5). Roll half of the dough into a 12 × 8-inch (30 × 20 cm) rectangle. Brush one-third of the melted chocolate mixture over the dough, covering evenly. Sprinkle dough with half of the pecan filling. Roll up the dough jelly-roll style, beginning from a long side; moisten edge with water and pinch to seal seam well. Slice the roll into twelve equal rounds. Repeat with remaining dough. Prepare Glaze; combine the brown sugar, butter, and corn syrup in a medium saucepan, over medium-high heat. Stir until butter is melted and sugar dissolved; stir in the pecans. Divide sauce evenly between two 9-inch (22.5 cm) round cake pans. Place rolls in prepared pans. Cover; let rise until nearly doubled in size, about 30 minutes. Place on center rack of oven and bake for 20 to 25 minutes or until golden brown. Remove from the oven and while warm invert onto a serving plate, and drizzle with remaining chocolate sauce.

Prep = 2 hours   **Cook** = 20 - 25 minutes   **Yield** = 2 dozen rolls

White Chocolate–Orange Scones with Dried Cranberries

These tender, delicious pastries are great for breakfast and perfect for afternoon tea.

2 1/2 cups (300 g) all-purpose flour
1/2 cup (48 g) sliced almonds, ground to cornmeal consistency
2 tablespoons (26 g) granulated sugar
1 tablespoon plus 1/2 teaspoon (16 g) baking powder
3/4 teaspoon salt
1/2 teaspoon ground cardamom
6 tablespoons (83 g) cold unsalted butter, cut into 1/2-inch (1.3 cm) cubes
2 eggs
1/2 cup (120 ml) heavy cream
1/4 teaspoon orange extract
1/2 cup (88 g) chopped white chocolate or chips
1/2 cup (83 g) dried cranberries
coarse sugar

Preheat oven to 375°F (190°C, or gas mark 5). Line a baking sheet with parchment paper. In a large mixing bowl, whisk together the flour, ground almonds, sugar, baking powder, salt, and cardamom. Using a pastry knife or two table knives, cut the butter into the flour mixture until it resembles cornmeal. In a small mixing bowl, whisk together the eggs, heavy cream, and orange extract. Pour all but 1/4 cup of liquid into the dry ingredients; add the chocolate and cranberries, stirring just to combine—do not overwork the dough. Turn out the dough onto a floured work surface, form into a ball, and knead a few times, until smooth, working in more flour if the dough seems too sticky. Press the dough into a 1-inch (2.5 cm) thick disk and cut into twelve equal wedges. Transfer wedges to the prepared baking sheet. Brush with remaining egg mixture and sprinkle with coarse sugar and remaining sliced almonds. Bake for 15 to 20 minutes, until the bottoms are golden brown and the tops are lightly browned. Transfer to a rack to cool. Serve warm with marmalade.

Variation: For a chocolate-chip scone replace 1/2 cup (88 g) white chocolate chips with 1/2 cup (88 g) milk chocolate chips.

Prep = 20 minutes **Cook** = 15 to 20 minutes **Yield** = 1 dozen scones

Chocolate Monkey Bread

Adapted from a Scharffen Berger chocolate recipe, this moist and delicious breakfast treat is also known as pull-apart bread or kuchen. Monkey Bread is a hybrid of doughnut holes and cinnamon rolls—individual bites of sweet bread covered in chocolate and nuts.

- ½ cup (120 ml) warm water (about 115°F [46°C])
- 2½ teaspoons active dry yeast
- 3 large egg yolks, lightly beaten
- 8 tablespoons (1 stick, or 112 g) unsalted butter, plus 8 tablespoons (1 stick, or 112 g) unsalted butter, melted
- ¾ cup (175 ml) whole milk
- ¼ teaspoon salt
- ⅓ cup (67 g) granulated sugar
- 4 cups (480 g) all-purpose flour
- ¾ cup (83 g) coarsely chopped pecans, toasted
- 4 ounces (115 g) coarsely chopped semisweet chocolate
- ½ cup (75 g) loosely packed light brown sugar

  Butter and sugar for the pan

In a small bowl, combine warm water and yeast, stirring to dissolve the yeast. Let stand for 10 minutes until the yeast is frothy.

Place the egg yolks in the bowl of a stand mixer fitted with the paddle attachment; beat on low just to break apart. In a small saucepan, melt 8 tablespoons (1 stick, or 112 g) butter with the whole milk, salt, and sugar. With the mixer running on low, gradually pour the butter mixture in with the egg yolks, beating to combine. Let stand for 10 minutes to cool a bit. Add the yeast mixture, mixing on low just to combine. Add half the flour, mixing on low just to combine. Add the remaining flour and mix just to combine. Increase the speed to medium and continue to beat until the dough is smooth, about 5 minutes. Coat a bowl with nonstick cooking spray, scrape out the dough into the bowl, turn once to coat with spray. Cover with a kitchen towel and let rise in a warm place for about 1½ hours, until doubled in size.

Place the pecans, chocolate, and brown sugar in a food processor and pulse until the mixture has a grainy consistency; set aside. Butter and dust with granulated sugar a 10-inch tube pan.

Pour 8 tablespoons of melted butter into a small bowl. Pull off small pieces of dough, rolling them into golf ball-size balls. Roll the balls in the melted butter, then in the nut-and-chocolate mixture to coat; place in the prepared pan. Continue this process with all of the dough, lining the bottom of the pan and working your way up, stacking like building blocks. Arrange the balls so that the top is even, making smaller balls if necessary. Cover with a kitchen towel and let rise again in a warm place for 1 hour, until doubled in size.

Preheat oven to 350°F (180°C, or gas mark 4). Brush the top of Monkey Bread with any remaining melted butter. Place on center rack of oven and bake for 45 to 50 minutes, until the top is dark brown and a skewer inserted in the center comes out clean. The insides of the Monkey Bread will be hot and steamy. Let stand in pan, cooling, for about 5 minutes, then turn out onto a wire rack and let cool for an additional 15 minutes. Serve warm.

Prep = 2½ hours **Cook** = 45 to 50 minutes **Chill** = 20 minutes
Yield = 10 servings

3

Puddings, Pies, and Tarts

Chocolate Chiffon Pie

Also called chocolate silk, this pie's texture is like a smooth, soft truffle.

   1   cup (120 g) chocolate wafer crumbs
 1/2   cup (63 g) ground hazelnuts
 1/4   cup (50 g) granulated sugar
   5   tablespoons (70 g) unsalted butter, melted

   1   cup (235 ml) whole milk
   2   teaspoons unflavored powdered gelatin
   2   eggs, separated
 1/2   cup (100 g) plus 2 tablespoons (26 g) granulated sugar
   8   ounces (225 g) semisweet chocolate, chopped
   1   teaspoon pure vanilla extract
   1   teaspoon hazelnut liqueur
 1/2   cup (50 g) cocoa nibs
1 1/2 cups (355 ml) heavy cream
   2   tablespoons (8 g) chopped hazelnuts for garnish

Preheat the oven to 400°F (200°C, or gas mark 6). For the crust, combine the chocolate crumbs, ground hazelnuts, 1/4 cup (50 g) sugar, and melted butter. Spoon into a 9-inch (22.5 cm) pie plate, pressing into the bottom and up the sides. Bake for 10 minutes. Allow to cool.

Place the milk in a heatproof bowl. Sprinkle the gelatin over the top, let it soften for 2 minutes. Place the bowl over a pot of boiling water. Beat the egg yolks with 1/4 cup (50 g) of the sugar and add to the milk with the chocolate. Stir until the gelatin has dissolved and the chocolate has melted. Remove from the heat, pour into the bowl of a stand mixer fitted with the blade attachment, and beat until smooth. Stir in the vanilla, hazelnut liqueur, and cocoa nibs; wrap and refrigerate for at least 1 hour. With a stand mixer and whisk attachment, whip the egg whites with the remaining 1/4 cup (50 g) sugar until soft peaks form. Fold the egg whites into the chocolate mixture until there are no white streaks. Clean the mixing bowl and whip the cream with the 2 tablespoons (25 g) sugar to soft peaks, then fold half of the whipped cream into the chocolate mixture, reserving the other half for decoration. Pour the filling into the pastry shell and refrigerate at least 3 hours, until set. Decorate with the remaining whipped cream and chopped hazelnuts, and serve.

Prep = 30 minutes   **Cook** = 10 minutes for crust   **Chill** = 3 hours
Yield = 8 servings

Chocolate Mascarpone Parfait with Mixed Berries

Parfaits are a great make-ahead dessert or brunch dish, especially if you appreciate charming your guests. Spoon the parfaits into tall glass stemware in the morning and top with toasted almonds just before serving.

3	cups (440 g) mixed berries (blueberries, sliced strawberries, raspberries)
1/3	cup (80 ml) orange liqueur
1	tablespoon (15 ml) fresh lemon juice
1/2	pound (225 g) mascarpone cheese
2	ounces (55 g) dark chocolate, melted
1/4	cup (50 g) granulated sugar
1	cup (235 ml) heavy whipping cream
1/2	cup (63 g) Chocolate Chip Granola (page 63)
1/2	cup (50 g) crumbled chocolate wafer cookies
2	tablespoons (12 g) sliced almonds, lightly toasted

In a bowl, stir the berries with the orange liqueur and lemon juice; set aside. Place the bowl of a stand mixer in the freezer to chill. In a large bowl, whisk together the mascarpone, melted chocolate, and sugar until well blended and smooth. In the chilled mixing bowl, whip the heavy cream until stiff peaks form. Using a rubber spatula, fold the whipped cream into the mascarpone mixture just until combined. Divide half of the mascarpone mixture among six parfait glasses. Spoon in the berries, then the crumbled chocolate cookies, followed by granola. Spoon on the remaining mascarpone mixture and cover each glass with plastic wrap. Refrigerate for at least 1 hour. When ready to serve, uncover, sprinkle with toasted almonds, and serve.

Prep = 30 minutes   **Cook** = 1 hour   **Yield** = 6 servings

Chocolate Panna Cotta

Panna cotta, which means "cooked cream," is a classic Italian gelatin dessert that is believed to have originated in northern Italy's Piedmont region. Typically made from milk and cream simmered with gelatin, panna cotta is served with mixed berries and fruits or fruit and chocolate sauce.

1 cup (235 ml) whole milk
1 tablespoon (7 g) unflavored powdered gelatin
3 cups (705 ml) heavy cream
4 heaping teaspoons instant espresso powder
2 ounces (55 g) grated bittersweet chocolate
1/2 cup (100 g) granulated sugar
Pinch of salt

CHOCOLATE SAUCE:
2 ounces (55 g) semisweet chocolate
2/3 cup (160 ml) light cream
Chocolate Curls (page 220)

Place the milk in a small saucepan and sprinkle with gelatin; let stand for 5 minutes while the gelatin softens. Place over medium heat and stir just until the gelatin dissolves, about 2 minutes. Add the cream, espresso powder, chocolate, sugar, and salt. Stir over low heat until the chocolate melts and the mixture becomes smooth, about 3 minutes. Remove from the heat and let cool. Pour the cream mixture into four martini glasses or ramekins, divided equally. Cover with plastic wrap and refrigerate until set, at least 6 hours and up to overnight.

For the Chocolate Sauce: Place the chocolate in a small bowl. Heat the cream in a saucepan over medium heat until it begins to steam. Pour the hot cream over the chocolate; let stand for 2 minutes, then stir until dissolved and smooth. Serve the panna cotta drizzled with chocolate sauce and topped with sweetened whipped cream and chocolate curls.

Prep = 10 minutes **Chill** = 6 hours **Yield** = 4 servings

White Chocolate–Strawberry Trifle

I have used the White Chocolate–Orange Pound Cake (page 147) for the cake layers, but a store-bought version or your favorite recipe will work just as well.

- 1 cup (165 g) dried tart cherries
- 1 pint (350 g) strawberries, hulled and sliced thin
- 1 tablespoon (13 g) granulated sugar
- 1 tablespoon (15 ml) fresh lemon juice
- 1½ cups (360 g) mascarpone cheese, softened
- 1 cup (235 ml) heavy cream
- 4 ounces (115 g) white chocolate
- 1 teaspoon orange extract
- 1 White Chocolate-Orange Pound Cake (page 147)
- ½ cup (120 ml) orange liqueur (such as Grand Marnier)
- 1 cup (235 ml) melted vanilla ice cream
- 1 cup (140 g) slivered almonds, plus 2 tablespoons, toasted, for garnish

Place the dried cherries in a small bowl and add boiling water to cover. Let stand for at least 30 minutes. Drain, and set aside at least 2 tablespoons (20 g) of cherries for garnish. Place the strawberries in a small bowl, sprinkle with sugar and lemon juice, turn to coat evenly, set aside. In a bowl, using a mixer on medium speed, beat the mascarpone and heavy cream until smooth, about 10 seconds. Place the white chocolate in the top of a double boiler over high heat and melt until smooth. With the mixer running on low, add the warm chocolate to the mascarpone mixture, blending until well combined, about 1 minute. Add orange extract and blend for 10 seconds.

In a 2½-quart (2.37 L) trifle dish, begin by breaking half of the pound cake into pieces and fit in an even layer. Drizzle the cake with half of the orange liqueur. Layer with half of the ice cream, then top with half of the strawberries and cherries. Top fruit with half of the mascarpone cheese mixture. Sprinkle the mascarpone with half of the toasted almonds. Repeat layers with remaining cake, orange liqueur, vanilla ice cream, fruit, and mascarpone cheese. Garnish with cherries and slivered almonds. Cover loosely with plastic wrap and refrigerate for at least 1 hour and up to 1 day before serving.

Prep = 40 minutes **Cook** = 1 hour **Yield** = 10 servings

Rum Cherry Bread Pudding with Chocolate Swirl

Everyone knows cherries and chocolate marry well. Here, combined with dark rum, the two take bread pudding to decadent matrimonial heights. Reserve the orange-rum soaking liquid to make a tasty glaze for each serving.

⅓	cup (80 ml) dark rum
⅓	cup (80 ml) orange juice
1	cup (165 g) dried cherries
5	ounces (140 g) bittersweet chocolate chips or squares chopped
1	cup (235 ml) heavy cream
8	tablespoons (1 stick, or 112 g) unsalted butter, sliced
1	loaf brioche or challah bread, torn into cubes (about 9 cups)
1½	cups (300 g) granulated sugar
4	eggs
2	egg yolks
1	tablespoon (15 ml) pure vanilla extract
3	cups (705 ml) whole milk
1	cup (100 g) confectioners' sugar

Preheat the oven to 325°F (170°C, or gas mark 3). Combine rum, orange juice, and cherries in a small saucepan; bring to a boil. Boil for 1 minute, transfer to a small bowl, set aside to cool for 30 minutes. Place chocolate in a small bowl. Place heavy cream in a small saucepan and bring to a boil; pour over chocolate, let stand for 3 minutes. After 3 minutes, stir cream and chocolate just to swirl and combine. Place butter in a 2-quart (2 L) casserole with at least 2-inch (5 cm) tall sides. Place in preheated oven and melt butter. Once butter is melted, remove from oven and toss torn bread with butter, coating evenly; set aside. In a large mixing bowl, whisk together the sugar, eggs, egg yolks, and vanilla until smooth. Add milk and whisk to combine. Drain cherries, reserving liquid. Spread cherries in and around bread. Add 1 tablespoon (15 ml) of the reserved liquid to milk mixture, stirring to combine. Pour milk mixture over bread, pressing bread

Prep = 30 minutes   **Cook** = 80 minutes   **Yield** = 12 servings

down with a spoon to allow liquid to cover; set aside for 10 minutes to soak. After 10 minutes, chocolate-and-cream mixture over bread, swirling the mixture into the bread just to incorporate. Sprinkle confectioners' sugar over entire pudding, coating evenly. Place casserole on the center rack of oven and bake for 1 hour 20 minutes, until firm.

Remove and let rest for 10 minutes. Serve warm with the Rum-Cherry Sauce.

RUM-CHERRY SAUCE:

Reserved soaking liquid from cherries plus water to make 1/2 cup (120 ml) liquid

1/2 **cup (100 g) granulated sugar**

2 **tablespoons (28 g) unsalted butter, chilled**

For the Rum-Cherry Sauce: Place cherry-rum liquid in a small saucepan, add sugar, and bring to a boil. Boil for 2 minutes; set aside to cool for 2 minutes. After 2 minutes, drop butter 1 tablespoon (14 g) at a time into sauce, whisking vigorously until combined. Drizzle glaze over each serving of bread pudding.

Chocolate Risotto Rice Pudding

Is there any dessert that is more of a comfort food than rice pudding? The classic, rich and creamy dish is only improved with the addition of dark chocolate. This simple recipe can be served warm right out of the oven or chilled, with whipped cream and shaved chocolate.

1	cup (200 g) Arborio rice
2	teaspoons salt
4	cups (945 ml) water
1	(13.5 ounce, or 378 ml) can unsweetened coconut milk
3	cups (710 ml) milk
4	large egg yolks
1/2	teaspoon pure vanilla extract
1/2	cup (120 ml) sweetened condensed milk
1/4	cup (60 g) firmly packed light brown sugar
3	ounces (85 g) bittersweet chocolate chips or squares, chopped

Preheat oven to 325°F (170°C, or gas mark 3). Lightly grease a 2-quart (2 L) casserole dish. In a large saucepan, combine the rice, salt, and water and bring to a boil over high heat. Boil for 5 minutes, remove from heat, and drain rice. Place rice back in saucepan, add coconut milk and milk, and simmer for 25 minutes, stirring occasionally until most of the milk is absorbed. In a small bowl, whisk the egg yolks with the vanilla, condensed milk, and brown sugar. Remove rice from heat and gradually temper the egg mixture by adding a small amount of the hot rice mixture to the egg mixture, stirring to combine. Add the warmed egg mixture gradually to the hot rice, stirring constantly. Add the chocolate and stir to combine and melt. Transfer rice to casserole, cover and bake for 40 minutes. Remove from oven and let cool. Cover with plastic wrap, and refrigerate for up to 3 days.

Prep = 30 minutes **Cook** = 40 minutes **Yield** = 10 servings

Chocolate Mint Crème Brûlée

Luscious crème brûlée may seem intimidating, but it is simple to make and elegant to serve. The custard base can be made up to two days ahead of time and the caramelized top finished at the table with a flourish, in front of your guests, using a kitchen torch.

    3   cups (710 ml) whipping cream
    1   cup (235 ml) whole milk
    ½   cup (100 g) granulated sugar
   12   fresh mint leaves
   1¼   cups (220 g) chopped dark chocolate
   1¼   cups (220 g) chopped milk chocolate
    8   egg yolks
    ½   cup (100 g) superfine sugar

Preheat the oven to 300°F (150°C, or gas mark 2). Butter eight (1-cup, or 235 ml) ramekins.

Put the cream, milk, sugar, and mint leaves in a saucepan and bring to a boil. Remove from heat and let sit for 30 minutes. Remove the mint leaves; reheat the mixture until steaming and bubbles form around the edge. Add the chocolates, stirring until smooth.

Using a stand mixer fitted with the paddle attachment, beat the egg yolks until smooth; gradually adding the chocolate mixture while beating on low to combine. Strain the custard into each of the prepared ramekins, filling about ½ inch (1.3 cm) from the top. Place the ramekins in a deep-sided roasting pan and place on center rack of oven. Add hot water to rise just halfway up the sides of the ramekins. Bake for 25 to 30 minutes, until the custard is set and a skewer inserted into the center of one comes out clean.

Remove from oven and transfer ramekins to a cooling rack to cool completely. Cover each with plastic wrap and refrigerate for at least 4 hours or overnight. When ready to serve, remove custards from the refrigerator and dab with a paper towel to remove any moisture that may have accumulated on the tops. Sprinkle each evenly with the sugar. Heat oven broiler or ignite a small kitchen blowtorch and heat the tops until the sugar has melted and caramelized. Serve immediately.

Prep = 20 minutes **Bake** = 25 to 30 minutes
Chill = At least 4 hours **Yield** = 8 servings

Chocolate Brioche Bread Pudding

In a word: fantastic. Bread pudding is good any way you make it. This recipe was intentionally kept simple, but feel free to add ½ cup (75 g) of raisins or nuts to the bread cubes along with the chocolate chips.

- 4 tablespoons (½ stick, or 55 g) butter
- 1 loaf day-old brioche, torn into pieces
- ½ cup (88 g) semisweet chocolate chips
- 3 cups (710 ml) whole milk
- 1 cup (235 ml) heavy cream
- 6 ounces (170 g) bittersweet chocolate, chopped finely
- 4 eggs
- ½ cup (100 g) granulated sugar, plus 1 tablespoon (13 g) for dusting
- ¾ teaspoon vanilla extract
- Pinch of nutmeg
- Pinch of salt

Preheat oven to 350°F (180°C, or gas mark 4). Place butter in a large oval or round casserole or baking dish with at least 3-inch (7.5 cm) high sides, place in oven to melt butter. Remove from oven and toss brioche in butter, coating pieces evenly. Sprinkle the bread with the chocolate chips and move around a bit just to incorporate the chips, set aside. Meanwhile, in a 2-quart (2 L) saucepan, heat the milk with the cream over medium heat just until the mixture foams and steam begins to rise. Add the chocolate, stirring to melt; set aside to cool slightly, about 10 minutes. In a large bowl, beat the eggs with the sugar, vanilla extract, nutmeg, and salt until creamy. Gradually whisk in the warmed milk mixture, beating constantly so as not to cook the eggs. Pour the combined mixture over the bread, pushing down on the bread cubes to submerge and coat them. Prepare a water bath by lining the bottom of a large roasting pan (large enough to hold the casserole) with a double layer of paper towels (this will keep the dish from sliding around). Place the casserole or dish on the towels. Pour hot water into the roasting pan to reach halfway up the sides of the casserole. Place the roasting pan with the casserole on the middle rack of the oven. Bake for 40 minutes, or until firm. Remove and serve warm.

Prep = 20 minutes **Cook** = 40 minutes
Yield = 10 servings

Caramel Peanut Butter Tart with Salted Almond Crust

This tart is a creamy, delicious delight with a sweet and salty crunch. I use coarse sea salt in the crust as it holds up better than table salt during baking, instead of disappearing into the other ingredients. It adds a pretzel-like flavor and bite to the crust.

FOR SALTED ALMOND CRUST:

- 1 cup (120 g) graham cracker crumbs
- 1 cup (125 g) ground Marcona almonds
- 2 tablespoons (26 g) granulated sugar
- 1 teaspoon sea salt
- 8 tablespoons (1 stick, or 112 g) unsalted butter, melted

FILLING:

- 2 large eggs
- 1 large egg yolk
- 2 teaspoons pure vanilla extract
- 1/2 cup (130 g) creamy peanut butter
- 1/4 teaspoon salt
- 1 1/2 cups (300 g) granulated sugar
- 1/2 cup (120 ml) water
- 1 1/4 cups (295 ml) heavy cream
- 1 1/2 cups (190 g) slivered almonds

GANACHE:

- 7 ounces (200 g) dark chocolate, chopped
- 3/4 cup (175 ml) heavy whipping cream
- 1/2 teaspoon pure vanilla extract

Preheat oven to 350°F (180°C, or gas mark 4).

Prepare the Salted Almond Crust: Combine the graham cracker crumbs, ground almonds, sugar, and salt. Add the butter and mix together. Press the mixture into the bottom and sides of a 9-inch (22.5 cm) tart pan. Bake for 10 minutes; remove from the oven and let cool.

For the Filling: Combine the eggs and yolk and whisk until creamy. Add the vanilla, peanut butter, salt, sugar, water, heavy cream, and almonds; stir to combine well. Pour mixture into tart shell. Place in oven and bake for 30 minutes, or until set. Remove and let cool.

For the Ganache: Place chocolate in a bowl and set aside. Heat the heavy cream in a saucepan over medium-high heat until steam rises and bubbles form around the edges. Pour over the chocolate; let sit for 1 minute, then stir until melted and smooth. Stir in the vanilla. Let cool for 15 minutes. Unmold the tart and place on a cake plate. Pour the ganache over the top, smoothing out. Refrigerate for at least 30 minutes, until ganache is set. Slice and serve.

Prep = 30 minutes **Cook** = 30 minutes **Yield** = 10 servings

Chocolate-Apricot Kolaches

Pronounced *koh-LAH-cheese*, these desserts are Polish in origin, whereas others argue they are Czech. Either way, I grew up eating them in Texas, filled with sausage. My version features chocolate dough and an apricot-preserves filling—take whatever liberties you like.

    1 (12-ounce, 340 g) jar apricot preserves
  1/2 cup (55 g) finely chopped pecans
  1/2 teaspoon ground cinnamon
  1/4 teaspoon ground nutmeg
  1/2 teaspoon pure vanilla extract
    1 cup (2 sticks, or 225 g) unsalted butter or margarine, softened
    1 (8-ounce, or 225 g) package cream cheese, softened
    2 tablespoons (26 g) granulated sugar
 1 1/2 cups (180 g) all-purpose flour
  1/2 cup (45 g) unsweetened cocoa powder
    1 large egg, beaten with 1 tablespoon water
  1/4 cup (25 g) confectioners' sugar sifted with 1/4 cup (23 g) cocoa powder

Preheat oven to 350°F (180°C, or gas mark 4). Spray a sheet pan with nonstick cooking spray. In a small bowl, stir together the apricot preserves, pecans, cinnamon, nutmeg, and vanilla; set aside. In the bowl of a stand mixer fitted with the paddle attachment, beat together the butter and cream cheese until smooth. Add sugar and beat to combine; add the flour and cocoa, beating on low just to combine. Divide dough in half and roll each half to 1/8-inch (0.3 cm) thickness. Using a 6-inch (15 cm) round cutter, cut out circles. Spoon 1 teaspoon of filling onto the center of each round. Brush around the edges of the dough with the egg wash. Fold the circles over, making half circles, and pinch the dough together around the edges. Place on prepared sheet pan and bake for 12 to 15 minutes until golden. Transfer to wire racks to cool. Sprinkle with mixture of confectioners' sugar and cocoa to serve.

Prep = 30 minutes **Cook** = 12 to 15 minutes
Yield = About 2 1/2 dozen

Milk Chocolate and Peanut Butter Pudding with Salted Cashew Candy

I paired "smooth and creamy" with "crunchy and salty" for layered texture and flavor. Like brittle, cashew candy is a great topper for ice cream or mousse, too.

³/₄	cup (150 g) granulated sugar
¹/₄	cup (25 g) cornstarch
¹/₃	cup (32 g) unsweetened cocoa powder
2¹/₂	cups (590 ml) whole milk
¹/₂	cup (120 ml) heavy cream
5	ounces (140 g) milk chocolate chips or squares, chopped
1¹/₂	teaspoons pure vanilla extract
1	teaspoon dark rum
¹/₄	cup (65 g) creamy peanut butter

CASHEW CANDY:

¹/₂	cup (100 g) sugar
2	tablespoons (28 ml) water
1	tablespoons (20 g) honey
¹/₂	cup (65 g) salted cashews
¹/₈	teaspoon ground nutmeg

In a saucepan, combine the sugar, cornstarch, cocoa, milk, and cream. Bring to a boil and then reduce heat to a simmer. Add the chocolate, stirring until smooth. Add the vanilla, dark rum, and peanut butter. Cook until mixture is thickened, about 5 minutes. Pour into a glass bowl and cover with plastic wrap, pressing the plastic directly on top of the pudding. Refrigerate until set, at least 3 hours.

To make the Cashew Candy: Place the sugar, water, and honey in a saucepan over medium-high heat and bring to a boil. Add the cashews and nutmeg and continue to boil for 5 minutes. Line a baking sheet with waxed paper, pour the mixture out onto the waxed paper, and let cool until hardened; break into pieces. Serve the chilled pudding in dessert cups topped with the cashew candy.

Prep = 30 minutes **Chill** = 3 hours
Yield = 4 servings

Toasted Coconut-Chocolate Chunk Pecan Pie

This pie features a beautiful crust and is packed with layers of flavors—coconut, chocolate, and pecans. Is it a pie or simply heaven? Try to find plump and tender pecans—they are the essential ingredient.

CRUST:
- ¼ cup (20 g) ground rolled oats (ground in food processor until they resemble cornmeal)
- 1 cup (120 g) all-purpose flour
- 1 tablespoon (13 g) granulated sugar
- ¼ teaspoon salt
- 8 tablespoons (1 stick, or 112 g) cold unsalted butter, cut into 1-inch (2.5 cm) cubes
- 3 tablespoons (45 ml) very cold water

- 1½ cups (150 g) pecan halves
- 4 ounces (115 g) dark chocolate, chopped finely
- ⅓ cup (75 g) butter or margarine
- 5 ounces (140 g) dark chocolate, chopped coarsely
- 1 cup (200 g) granulated sugar
- 1 cup (320 g) light corn syrup
- 4 large eggs, lightly beaten
- 1 teaspoon pure vanilla extract
- ¼ teaspoon salt
- 1 cup (70 g) sweetened flaked coconut, toasted

COCOA WHIPPED CREAM:
- 1 tablespoon (13 g) granulated sugar
- 1 tablespoon (6 g) unsweetened cocoa powder
- ¾ cup (175 ml) very cold heavy cream

(Continued on page 98)

(Continued from page 96)

For the Crust: In the bowl of a food processor, combine oats, flour, sugar, and salt; pulse a couple of times to combine. Add the butter and pulse until mixture resembles fine cornmeal. Add the cold water and blend until the dough forms a ball. Turn out dough onto a dry work surface and form into a disk. Wrap in plastic wrap and refrigerate for 2 hours. Remove dough from refrigerator and place on a floured work surface, then roll out to a 12-inch (30.5 cm) circle. Transfer dough to a 9-inch (22.9 cm) pie plate, crimping the edges.

Preheat oven to 350°F (180°C, or gas mark 4).

Prick dough with the tines of a fork all over the bottom. Line dough with foil and cover with pastry weights or dried beans or rice. Bake for 20 minutes, just until it begins to brown. Remove crust from oven and let cool completely. Once cool, top crust with pecan halves and finely chopped chocolate. In a large saucepan over low heat, melt the butter with the coarsely chopped dark chocolate. Add the sugar, corn syrup, eggs, vanilla, and salt; stir until the sugar is dissolved. Remove from heat, and stir in coconut. Pour mixture over pecans and chocolate in crust. Place pie on the center rack of oven and bake for 45 to 50 minutes, until the top is golden brown and has set. Remove and let cool for 20 minutes; slice and serve with cocoa whipped cream.

For the Cocoa Whipped Cream: Place the bowl of a stand mixer in the freezer for 15 minutes. Stir together the sugar and cocoa powder. Working with the mixer fitted with the whisk attachment, whip the cream in the chilled bowl until foamy, about 2 minutes. Add the cocoa sugar and continue to beat until soft peaks form. Use immediately or store refrigerated for up to 1 hour.

Prep = 2 hours   **Cook** = 45 to 50 minutes   **Yield** = 10 servings

Classic Chocolate Mousse

This could not be a book on chocolate without a recipe for Classic Chocolate Mousse. Because of its restaurant-quality reputation, it is thought to be difficult and time consuming. It is quite the opposite. With only five ingredients and a little mixing, the refrigeration is the most time-consuming part of the dish. Six hours of refrigeration are needed for the mousse to set up properly, so if you are planning a lovely dinner party or luncheon, make it the day ahead.

8 ounces (225 g) bittersweet chocolate, chopped
6 tablespoons (83 g) unsalted butter, softened
6 eggs, separated
¼ teaspoon salt
¼ cup (25 g) confectioners' sugar

Place the chocolate in the top of a double boiler and melt. Add the butter and continue to stir until smooth. Working quickly, whisk 1 egg yolk at a time into the chocolate until well combined. Repeat until all are incorporated. Remove from the double boiler and set aside to cool. Add the salt to the reserved egg whites. Using a stand mixer fitted with the whisk attachment, whip the egg whites until stiff peaks form. Add the sugar and beat in. Using a rubber spatula, gently fold the egg whites into the chocolate mixture until there are no white streaks. Spoon the mixture into individual cocktail (martini) glasses or dessert cups. Cover and refrigerate for at least 6 hours or overnight. Serve cold, sprinkled with chocolate shavings.

Prep = 20 minutes **Cook** = at least 6 hours **Yield** = 6 servings

Truffle Tart with Shortbread Crust

Truffles are so rich and decadent that it only seemed right to add the same creamy texture to a tart with a sweet shortbread crust. The nuttiness of pecans in the crust is like rolling truffles in chopped pecans. While tempting right out of the oven, give this tart plenty of time to chill and set before serving. Dollop with some fresh whipped cream spiked with cinnamon and serve.

CRUST:

- 8 tablespoons (1 stick, or 112 g) unsalted butter, softened
- 2 cups (250 g) ground shortbread cookies
- 1/2 cup (60 g) all-purpose flour
- 1/2 cup (55 g) finely chopped pecans
- 1 large egg

FILLING:

- 2 ounces (55 g) bittersweet chocolate, melted
- 1/2 cup (75 g) crushed toffee candy
- 1/3 cup (80 ml) heavy cream
- 6 tablespoons (83 g) unsalted butter, softened
- 4 ounces (115 g) bittersweet chocolate, chopped
- 4 ounces (115 g) milk chocolate, chopped
- 2 large eggs, lightly beaten
- 1/4 cup (50 g) granulated sugar
- 1/4 teaspoon salt
- 1 teaspoon pure vanilla extract

For Crust: In the bowl of a stand mixer fitted with the paddle attachment, beat the butter with 1 cup (125 g) of shortbread crumbs on low speed until creamy. Beat in the flour, pecans, and egg. Add the remaining 1 cup (125 g) of shortbread crumbs and beat just to combine. Flatten the dough into a small disk between two sheets of plastic wrap and refrigerate for at least 30 minutes.

Preheat oven to 350°F (180°C, or gas mark 4). Working on a flour-dusted surface, roll out the dough to a 12-inch (30 cm) round. Lift the dough into a 10-inch (25 cm) fluted round tart pan, pressing the dough against the bottom and into the fluted edges. Trim away any excess around the edges. Refrigerate for at least 30 minutes. Line the shell with foil or parchment paper and fill with pie weights or dried beans or rice. Bake for 30 minutes, or until nearly set. Remove the foil and bake for an additional 10 minutes, until golden and aromatic. Remove tart shell from oven and let it cool completely. Brush the bottom and sides of the shell with the melted chocolate and sprinkle evenly with the crushed toffee candy. Refrigerate to set for 10 minutes.

For the Filling: In a medium saucepan, heat the cream until steam rises and bubbles begin to form around the edges; add the butter and allow to melt. Remove from heat, and add the bittersweet and milk chocolate; let stand for 2 minutes, then stir until smooth. In a bowl, whisk together the eggs, sugar, salt, and vanilla. Gradually pour the chocolate mixture into the egg mixture, stirring constantly. Pour the filling into the tart shell, spreading evenly. Bake for 20 to 25 minutes, or until set. Remove and let cool completely. Refrigerate for at least 4 hours before slicing to serve.

Prep = 1 hour 40 minutes **Cook** = 40 minutes for crust,
20 to 25 minutes for tart **Chill** = 4 hours **Yield** = 10 servings

---

White Chocolate Cherry Tart with Shortbread Crust

Graham cracker crust is the granddaddy of all tart crusts, but browsing the cookie and cracker aisle of the grocery store will yield numerous options for unique crusts. For this tart, shortbread cookies are the star (though use any you like). The amount of butter already in shortbread cookies make them ideal. (Consider using the Browned Butter Shortbread Cookies on page 18.)

PASTRY:

- 1 cup (120 g) all-purpose flour
- ³/₄ cup (95 g) ground shortbread cookies (about 8 cookies)
- ¹/₄ cup (50 g) granulated sugar
- 6 tablespoons (83 g) cold unsalted butter, cut into small pieces
- 1 egg yolk
- 3 tablespoons (45 ml) heavy whipping cream
- 1 tablespoon (15 ml) orange liqueur (such as Grand Marnier or orange Curaçao)
- 1 tablespoon (5 g) grated orange zest
- ¹/₂ cup (63 g) finely chopped hazelnuts

FILLING:

- 5 ounces (140 g) white chocolate, melted
- 1¹/₂ cups (360 g) mascarpone cheese, softened
- ¹/₂ cup (100 g) sugar
- 1 egg
- 3 egg yolks
- Zest of 1 orange (about 1 tablespoon [6 g])
- 1 tablespoon (15 ml) orange liqueur
- ¹/₂ teaspoon ground cardamom
- ¹/₂ cup (160 g) sour cherry jam
- 1 cup (235 ml) Morello cherries (in syrup, drained)
- Confectioners' sugar for dusting

Prepare the Pastry: In the bowl of a food processor fitted with the blade attachment, combine the flour, shortbread cookies, and sugar; pulse to combine. Add the butter and blend until the texture resembles coarse meal. Ad the egg yolk, cream, liqueur, and zest and blend until the dough comes together into a ball. Remove and form into an 8-inch (20 cm) disk. Wrap in plastic wrap and chill for at least 1 hour.

Preheat oven to 400°F (200°C, or gas mark 6). Remove dough from the refrigerator and let sit for 10 minutes. Dust a dry, flat surface with flour. Place dough on floured work surface and roll out into a 12-inch (30 cm) circle, just to fit the tart pan and come up the sides, turning and dusting with flour as needed. Using the bottom circle of the tart pan, gently slide the disk under the dough to the center, making it easier to pick up the dough and transfer it to the tart pan. Gently place the dough in the tart pan, pressing up the sides of the pan. Using your finger, gently press away any excess dough around the edges, using extra dough to fill in any voids. Sprinkle the hazelnuts over the dough evenly, gently pressing into the dough. Line the dough with foil and weight with dry beans, rice, or pastry weights. Bake on the center rack of the oven for 15 minutes. Reduce heat to 350°F (180°C, or gas mark 4) and continue to bake until dough is firm and golden brown, about 15 additional minutes. Remove from the oven and let cool uncovered for 20 minutes.

Reduce oven temperature to 325°F (170°C, or gas mark 3).

For the Filling: In the top of a double boiler set over boiling water, melt the white chocolate; set aside for 5 minutes. Using a stand mixer fitted with the paddle attachment or a hand mixer, blend the mascarpone cheese, sugar, egg and yolks, orange zest and liqueur, and cardamom together until combined. With the mixer running on low speed, add the white chocolate in a steady stream to prevent hardening. Blend until just combined.

Once the pastry crust has cooled, spread the cherry jam over the crust, topping it with a layer of the cherries. Pour the filling over the cherries, spreading in an even layer. Bake the tart on the middle rack for 45 to 50 minutes, until set and the top is golden. Remove from oven, let cool for 20 minutes, remove tart from the pan and allow to cool completely. Dust with confectioners' sugar and serve.

Prep = 1 hour **Cook** = 50 minutes **Chill** = 30 minutes
Yield = 12 servings

Chocolate-Chili Espresso Pots de Crème

A classic French dessert, pots de crème are what the name implies: pots of velvety, rich cream or custard. This marriage of chocolate and espresso conceals a punchy surprise of chili powder, which add a salty crunch.

6	ounces (170 g) fine quality bittersweet chocolate, chopped finely
1½	cups (355 ml) heavy cream
⅓	cup (80 ml) whole milk
1½	tablespoons (15 g) instant espresso powder
6	large egg yolks
3	tablespoons (39 g) granulated sugar
½	teaspoon ancho chili powder
¼	cup (60 ml) brandy
1½	teaspoons vanilla extract

CHILI PEPPER PECANS:

1	tablespoon (14 g) butter
⅓	cup (37 g) roughly chopped pecans
1	tablespoon (15 g) firmly packed brown sugar
⅛	teaspoon ancho chili powder
	Pinch of cayenne
	Pinch of salt and black pepper
¼	teaspoon granulated sugar

Preheat oven to 300°F (150°C, or gas mark 2) and position rack in center. Prepare a deep-sided roasting pan by layering a double thickness of paper towels on the bottom. Place six 4-ounce, (120 ml), custard cups, ramekins, or pot de creme cups in the pan. Bring 4 cups (945 ml) water to a boil, set aside.

Place chocolate in a heatproof bowl. In a large saucepan over medium-high heat, heat the cream with the milk just until boiling; add the espresso powder, stir to dissolve. Pour half of the cream mixture over the chocolate, stirring with a wooden spoon or rubber spatula until chocolate is melted and the ganache is smooth. In a mixing bowl, whisk the egg yolks with the sugar and chili powder until creamy and smooth. Gradually, in a slow, steady stream, whisking all the while, pour the remaining warmed milk mixture over the egg mixture to combine. Add the hot liquid slowly as this will temper the eggs, thickening the mixture without scrambling the eggs. Stir in the brandy and vanilla. Slowly pour the egg mixture into the melted chocolate, stirring gently to combine. Using a spoon, skim any foam from the top of the custard.

(Continued on page 106)

(Continued from page 104)

Divide the custard evenly among cups. Pour enough of the hot water in the pan to rise halfway up the sides of the cups. Cover pan tightly with aluminum foil, piercing a few holes around the top of the foil. If using pots de creme cups with their own lids, those lids are enough for a cover. Carefully place the pan in the oven. Bake until custards are set around edges but still have movement to them, 30 to 40 minutes. Gently remove from the oven and let rest in pan, covered for 10 minutes. Uncover and transfer ramekins to a cooling rack for 1 hour. Pots de crème may be served at room temperature, or if you prefer, cover with plastic wrap and chill until cold throughout, at least 3 hours.

For the Chili Pepper Pecans: Melt the butter in a medium skillet over medium heat. Add the pecans, brown sugar, chili powder, cayenne, salt, and black pepper. Stir pecans with spices until well coated and toasted, being careful not to burn them. Transfer the pecans to a sheet of aluminum foil or parchment paper, sprinkle with sugar and allow to cool. When ready to serve, crumble the pecans over the top of each custard.

Prep = 15 minutes **Cook** = 40 minutes **Yield** = 6 servings

White Chocolate Mousse

Velvety and smooth, this white chocolate mousse sparkles with orange flavor. It is an elegant and simple dessert presentation. To alter the flavor, replace the orange liqueur with hazelnut liqueur such as Frangelico and garnish with toasted, chopped hazelnuts.

2 cups (350 g) chopped white chocolate
4 large eggs, separated
1 tablespoon (15 ml) warm milk
3 cups (710 ml) whipping cream
1 tablespoon (13 g) granulated sugar
2 tablespoons (28 ml) orange liqueur, (such as Grand Marnier or Cointreau)
Grated zest of 1 orange
White chocolate curls (page 220)

In the top of a double boiler, melt the chocolate; set aside. In a the bowl of a stand mixer fitted with the whisk attachment, whip the egg yolks until pale yellow in color and increased in volume, about 3 minutes. With the mixer running on low speed, gradually add the chocolate in a steady stream. Once all the chocolate is in, add the warm milk, beating continuously until smooth and creamy; set mixture aside to cool.

Using a clean whisk attachment and a clean, dry bowl, whip the cream until soft peaks form. Reserve one-third of the cream in a separate bowl. Using a rubber spatula, gently fold the remaining cream into the chocolate mixture. Using a clean whisk attachment again, whip the egg whites and the sugar in a clean, dry bowl until soft peaks form. Using a rubber spatula, fold this mixture into the chocolate mixture as well, then fold in the orange liqueur and half the orange zest. Spoon the mousse into 6 to 8 individual 1-cup (235 ml) serving dishes, cover tightly with plastic wrap, and refrigerate for 24 hours before serving. Garnish the mousse with dollops of reserved whipped cream, orange zest, and chocolate curls.

Prep = 20 minutes **Chill** = 24 hours **Yield** = 6 to 8 servings

Mocha Hazelnut Chocolate Soufflé

Finely chopping the toasted hazelnuts allows their rich, nutty flavor to meld. You can bake these soufflés in 1 cup (235 ml) stainless steel measuring cups, preparing them just as you would the ramekins.

Unsweetened cocoa powder for dusting
3/4 cup (175 ml) whole milk
1/2 cup (120 ml) whipping cream
3 tablespoons (30 g) instant espresso powder
5 large eggs, separated
12 tablespoons (1 1/2 sticks, or 167 g) unsalted butter
1/2 cup (60 g) all-purpose flour, sifted
5 ounces (140 g) finely chopped dark chocolate
1 teaspoon hazelnut liqueur (such as Frangelico)
1/4 cup (50 g) granulated sugar
1/3 cup (42 g) finely chopped toasted hazelnuts
1 milk chocolate candy bar, broken into 6 pieces
Confectioners' sugar for dusting

Preheat oven to 400°F (200°C, or gas mark 6). Butter the sides and bottoms of ramekins, then dust with cocoa powder, shaking out excess. Heat the milk and cream in a saucepan over medium heat, just until steaming and bubbles form around the sides. Add the espresso powder, stir to dissolve, and set aside. Whisk the egg yolks in a bowl just to loosen. Melt the butter in a small saucepan and stir in the flour until well combined. Gradually pour the warm milk mixture in with the flour mixture, whisking until smooth. Remove from heat, add the dark chocolate, egg yolks, and liqueur, stirring to combine.

With a stand mixer and whisk attachment, whip the egg whites with the sugar until stiff peaks form, about 3 minutes. Using a rubber spatula, gently fold in half the egg whites into the chocolate mixture until just combined. Add the hazelnuts with the remaining egg whites and gently fold. Spoon about 1 tablespoon of the soufflé mixture into the six prepared ramekins, covering the bottoms. Add a piece of broken chocolate bar to each ramekin, then fill each to the top with remaining mixture, smoothing out the surface. Place the ramekins on a sheet pan and place on the center rack of the oven, baking for 15 to 20 minutes, until firm on top and risen. Serve warm, right out of the oven, with a dusting of confectioners' sugar.

Prep = 30 minutes **Cook** = 15 to 20 minutes **Yield** = 6 servings

Chocolate-Cherry Fried Pies

In the Texas Hill Country lies a famous little bakery—the Rather Sweet Bakery—famous for spectacular desserts and pastries. One of their most popular offerings is their fried pies, a famous Southern treat. My version contains the delicious combination of chocolate and cherries.

   ½ cup (88 g) chopped premium dark chocolate
   ½ cup (70 g) chopped milk chocolate
   ½ cup (160 g) cherry preserves

DOUGH:
   6 cups (720 g) all-purpose flour
   4 teaspoons (18 g) baking powder
   1 tablespoon (13 g) salt
   1 cup (2 sticks, or 225 g) unsalted butter, chilled and diced
   1½ cups (355 ml) ice water
      Peanut oil, for deep-frying

GLAZE:
   1 cup (100 g) confectioners' sugar
   2 tablespoons (28 ml) milk
   ½ teaspoon pure vanilla extract

In a bowl, combine the dark and milk chocolate with the cherry preserves.

To make the dough: Combine the flour, baking powder, and salt in a large mixing bowl. Using a pastry blender, cut the cold butter into the flour mixture until it resembles cornmeal. Add the ice water, working to combine. Gently form the dough into a ball and divide into three pieces. Dust a flat, dry work surface with flour. Roll out each portion of dough to ¹⁄₁₆-inch (0.2 cm) thickness. Cut out dough circles with a 5-inch (13 cm) round cutter. Each ball of dough should make four rounds.

Prep = 30 minutes   **Cook** = 5 minutes   **Yield** = 12 individual pies

Put 1 tablespoon (20 g) of filling in the center of each dough round. Fold the dough in half. Wet your fingers and press to seal the edges with water. Using a fork, crimp the edges of the pastry with the tines, being careful not to pierce the dough.

Pour about 3 inches (7.5 cm) oil into a deep-frying pan set over medium-high heat. Heat the oil to 325°F (170°C, or gas mark 3) (hot enough that a piece of dough dropped into the oil sizzles). Drop the pies a couple at a time into the oil and fry until floating and golden brown, about 2 to 3 minutes per side. Drain the pies on paper towels. Meanwhile, prepare the glaze. To make the glaze: Combine confectioners' sugar, milk, and vanilla with a whisk or a fork to make a smooth glaze. Glaze the warm pies and serve.

Variation:
Chocolate Cinnamon Fried Pies: Replace dark chocolates with same quantity Mexican chocolate. Instead of cherry preserves use apple preserves and add $1/2$ teaspoon ground cinnamon.

White Chocolate Ginger Peach: Omit dark and milk chocolate, add $1/2$ cup (88 g) chopped white chocolate. Replace cherry preserves with ginger preserves and add 2 white peaches, peeled and chopped.

4

Cakes and Tortes

Fudgy Chocolate Cake

This is more giant brownie than cake, with its assertive chocolate flavor and dense, luscious texture. Bake this in a cake pan or as individual cakes or cupcakes. For an even more lavish dessert, prepare a batch of Ganache (page 223) and pour it over the top before serving.

1	cup (2 sticks, or 225 g) unsalted butter
1/2	cup (45 g) unsweetened cocoa powder
3/4	cup (175 ml) water
5	ounces (140 g) dark chocolate, chopped
1	cup (200 g) granulated sugar
1	cup (225 g) lightly packed light brown sugar
3	large eggs
1/2	cup (120 ml) heavy whipping cream
1/2	cup (120 ml) whole milk
1	tablespoon (15 ml) pure vanilla extract
1 1/2	teaspoons baking powder
1/4	teaspoon salt
1 1/2	teaspoons ground cinnamon
1/4	teaspoon ground nutmeg
1 1/2	cups (180 g) all-purpose flour

Preheat oven to 325°F (170°C, or gas mark 3). Butter the sides and bottom of a 9-inch springform pan or spray with nonstick cooking spray. In a large saucepan over medium-high heat, melt the butter with the cocoa powder and water until creamy. Add the chocolate, stirring until melted. Add sugars, stirring until they are dissolved. Add the eggs one at a time, stirring vigorously after each addition to combine. Add the heavy cream, milk, vanilla, baking powder, salt, cinnamon, and nutmeg, stirring to combine. Add the flour 1/2 cup (60 g) at a time, stirring after each addition just to combine. Pour the batter into prepared baking pan. Bake for 60 to 70 minutes, until a wooden skewer inserted into the center comes out clean. Remove from oven and let cool for 5 minutes. Remove the sides of pan and let cool completely. Place on a cake plate and serve.

Prep = 20 minute **Cook** = 60 to 70 minutes **Cook** = 1 hour
Yield = 10 to 12 servings

Cashew Brownie Cake

The crunch and saltiness of cashews meet their perfect mate in chocolate. This cake, adapted from a recipe in Dorie Greenspan's *Baking*, is a sumptuous chocolate delight with the creaminess of cashew butter and the salty crunch of caramel-coated cashews.

- 1 cup (120 g) all-purpose flour
- 1/4 cup (23 g) unsweetened cocoa powder
- 1 teaspoon baking soda
- 1/4 teaspoon salt
- 1/8 teaspoon ground nutmeg
- 1 teaspoon cinnamon
- 5 ounces (140 g) bittersweet chocolate, chopped coarsley
- 8 tablespoons (1 stick, or 112 g) unsalted butter, cut into 8 pieces
- 4 eggs
- 1/2 cup (115 g) packed light brown sugar
- 1/4 cup (50 g) granulated sugar
- 3 tablespoons (60 g) light corn syrup
- 1/3 cup (87 g) all-natural cashew butter (or crunchy peanut butter)
- 1 teaspoon pure vanilla extract
- 1/2 cup (88 g) coarsley chopped semisweet chocolate, or chocolate chips

TOPPING:
- 2 cups (400 g) granulated sugar
- 1/2 cup (120 ml) water
- 1 1/2 tablespoons (30 g) light corn syrup
- 2/3 cup (160 ml) heavy cream
- 1 tablespoon (15 g) sour cream
- 2 tablespoons (28 g) unsalted butter, at room temperature
- 1 1/2 cups (195 g) salted cashews

(Continued on page 116)

(Continued from page 114)

Preheat oven to 350°F (180°C, or gas mark 4) and place a rack in the center. Butter sides and bottom of an 8-inch (20 cm) round springform pan and dust with flour, tapping out any excess.

Whisk together the flour, cocoa powder, baking soda, salt, nutmeg, and cinnamon in a mixing bowl; set aside. Prepare a double boiler over high heat. Melt the chocolate with the butter just until melted; set aside. In a large bowl, whisk the eggs with the sugars until well blended. Add the corn syrup, cashew butter, and vanilla, stirring to combine. Whisk in the melted butter and chocolate. Gradually add the dry ingredients, mixing only until just combined. Add the chopped chocolate and stir just to incorporate. Scrape the batter into the prepared pan and shake to even out.

Bake for 40 to 45 minutes, until a skewer inserted in the center comes out almost clean. Transfer pan to a cooling rack for 20 minutes. Run a knife along edges of the cake to release from pan. Remove the pan sides; let the cake cool completely. When cooled, invert the cake onto a cake plate and remove the pan bottom.

Meanwhile, prepare the topping. In a medium saucepan, combine the sugar, water, and corn syrup. Place the pan over medium-high heat; heat the caramel without stirring until it turns a rich amber color, 5 to 7 minutes. While heating, wipe down the inside of the pan as the caramel heats with a wet pastry brush to prevent any crystals from forming. Lower the heat and add the cream, sour cream, and butter—there may be some splattering, so be cautious of the hot liquids and steam. Stir to dissolve any lumps.

Add the cashews, stirring to incorporate. Pour the caramel into a glass measuring cup or mixing bowl and set aside to cool for 10 minutes. Spoon the nuts over the top of the cake and drizzle with remaining caramel, using as much or as little as you like. There will be an excess of caramel, so you can certainly save some for each portion of cake you serve. If you make the caramel too far in advance, it will harden too much. Simply submerge the glass measuring cup or bowl into a saucepan of hot water and bring to a boil to soften the caramel.

Prep = 30 minutes   **Cook** = 45 minutes   **Chill** = 30 minutes
Yield = 6 to 8 servings

Chocolate Chip Hazelnut Cake

I could not resist adapting this delightful cake from Williams-Sonoma's *Savoring Desserts*. By adding a topping of chocolate chips, the delicious flavor of pure hazelnuts is enhanced with a layer of chocolate goodness.

  2 cups (270 g) hazelnuts
1¼ cups (250 g) sugar
  ⅓ cup (40 g) all-purpose flour
  8 egg whites, at room temperature
  ½ teaspoon salt
  1 teaspoon pure vanilla extract
  1 cup (175 g) bittersweet chocolate chips

Preheat oven to 350°F (180°C, or gas mark 4). Butter and flour the bottom and sides of a 9-inch (22.9 cm) springform pan. In a food processor fitted with the blade attachment, combine the nuts with ½ cup (100 g) of the sugar and process until finely chopped. Add the flour and pulse to blend. Transfer mixture to a large mixing bowl and set aside. In the bowl of a stand mixer fitted with the paddle attachment, beat the egg whites and salt until foamy. Increase the speed to high and gradually beat in the remaining ¾ cup (150 g) of sugar until soft peaks form. Add the vanilla and beat until stiff, about 2 minutes longer. Using a rubber spatula, fold about half of the egg whites into the flour mixture, just to combine. Add the remaining egg whites and fold until there are no longer any white streaks. Pour the mixture into the prepared pan. Gently sprinkle the chocolate chips over the top in an even layer. Bake for 55 minutes, until a wooden skewer inserted into the center comes out clean (there may be a streak of chocolate as you pull through the chocolate chips, but there should be no batter). Transfer to a wire rack to cool for 10 minutes. Release the sides of the pan and slide the cake off of the base onto the rack to cool completely.

Prep = 30 minutes **Chill** = 10 minutes
Yield = 8 servings

Flourless Chocolate Almond Cake

I adapted this from a great recipe in Maureen McKeon's book *Crave: A Passion for Chocolate.*

 2   cups (350 g) chopped dark chocolate
 1/3 cup (75 g) unsalted butter
 7   large eggs, separated
 1/2 teaspoon cream of tartar
 1/2 cup (100 g) granulated sugar
 1   tablespoon (15 ml) dark rum
 3/4 cup (75 g) ground almonds

CHOCOLATE GLAZE:
 1 1/3 cups (228 g) chopped dark chocolate
 8   tablespoons (1/2 cup, or 112 g) unsalted butter
 2   tablespoons (28 ml) half-and-half
 1/3 cup (42 g) chopped toasted almonds, for garnish

Preheat oven to 325°F (170°C, or gas mark 3). Butter a 9-inch (22.5 cm) springform pan and line with parchment paper. Melt the chocolate and butter in the top of a double boiler; remove from heat and cool. Place the egg yolks in the bowl of stand mixer with a whisk attachment and beat for 2 minutes, until pale and thick—a ribbon should form when the beater is lifted from the mixture. Using a clean bowl and whisk attachment, whip the egg whites and cream of tartar until soft peaks form. Gradually add the sugar while beating. Continue to beat until stiff peaks form. Combine the egg yolks with the melted chocolate and rum and beat to combine. Working with a spatula, fold half the egg white mixture into the chocolate mixture. Add the remaining egg white mixture, folding until there are no white streaks; gently fold in the ground almonds. Pour the mixture into the prepared pan and bake for 50 to 55 minutes; the cake will begin to pull away from the sides. Transfer to a wire rack to cool before unmolding.

For Chocolate Glaze: Melt the chocolate, butter, and half-and-half in the top of a double boiler, stirring until smooth. Allow to cool until it becomes spreadable. Place the cake on a decorative cake plate and spread with glaze. Garnish the sides with chopped almonds.

Prep = 20 minutes **Cook** = 50 to 55 minutes
Yield = 8 servings

Chocolate Cupcake Cones

These are a clever way to craft individual servings for birthday parties. Make them ahead of time and then set up a decorating table with plenty of frosting and toppings so guests can create their own masterpieces. If you prefer regular cupcakes, use paper or aluminum cupcake cups in the muffin tins and fill them three-quarters full with batter. Bake the same amount of time.

1³⁄₄ cups (210 g) all-purpose flour
¹⁄₂ cup (45 g) unsweetened cocoa powder
2 teaspoons baking powder
¹⁄₂ teaspoon salt
12 tablespoons (1 ¹⁄₂ sticks, or 167 g) unsalted butter, softened
1¹⁄₄ cups (250 g) granulated sugar
2 eggs
2 ounces (55 g) dark chocolate, melted
1 cup (235 ml) whole milk
24 flat-bottomed ice-cream cones
1 recipe Chocolate Yum Yum Filling (page 230)
Sprinkles for garnish

In a mixing bowl whisk together the flour, cocoa powder, baking powder, and salt; set aside. In the bowl of a stand mixer fitted with the paddle attachment, beat the butter with the sugar until smooth and creamy, about 4 minutes. Add the eggs one at a time, beating well after each addition. Add the melted chocolate, beating to combine. Scrape the sides of the bowl. Add the flour mixture 1 cup (120 g) at a time, alternating with the milk, beginning and ending with the flour. Place the ice-cream cones in twelve muffin tins and fill half full with batter. Bake for 20 minutes or until cake springs back. Remove from the oven and allow to cool completely.

Fill a pastry bag with Chocolate Yum Yum Filling. Using a pastry bag fitted with the star tip, poke the tip into each cupcake, squeezing the filling into the cupcake, withdrawing the tip as you go and creating a star on top. Decorate with sprinkles and serve.

Prep = 20 minutes   **Cook** = 20 minutes   **Chill** = 1 hour
Yield = 24 cupcake cones

Classic German's Chocolate Cake

Not originating in Germany at all, this classic chocolate dessert was first introduced in 1957 by a Dallas homemaker who submitted it to run in a local newspaper. If you can't find German's Sweet Chocolate, use semisweet chocolate instead. This recipe yields plenty of the creamy coconut frosting, so be generous when spreading it around.

1	(4-ounce, 115 g) package German's Sweet Chocolate, chopped coarsely
⅓	cup (80 ml) half-and-half
1⅓	cups (160 g) all-purpose flour
⅓	cup (30 g) unsweetened cocoa powder
1	teaspoon baking soda
½	teaspoon salt
8	tablespoons (½ cup, or 112 g) butter or margarine
1	cup (200 g) granulated sugar
1	teaspoon pure vanilla extract
3	eggs, separated
⅔	cup (160 ml) buttermilk

COCONUT FROSTING:

2	eggs
1⅓	cups (267 g) granulated sugar
2	(5 ⅓-ounce, or 150 ml) cans evaporated milk
8	tablespoons (1 stick, or 112 g) butter or margarine
2½	cups (175 g) flaked coconut
1	cup (110 g) chopped pecans

Preheat oven to 350°F (180°C, or gas mark 4). Grease and flour two 8-inch (20 cm) round cake pans. In a saucepan, combine chocolate and half-and-half and heat until the chocolate is melted; set aside to cool. In a mixing bowl, whisk together the flour, cocoa powder, baking soda, and salt. In the bowl of stand mixer fitted with the paddle attachment, blend the butter, sugar, and vanilla on medium speed until creamy and smooth. Add the egg yolks one at a time, beating well after each addition. Scrape the sides of the bowl, add the melted chocolate, and beat to combine. Add the dry ingredients and buttermilk alternately, beating after each addition. In a clean mixing bowl with the whisk attachment, beat the egg whites until stiff peaks form. Fold the egg whites into the chocolate mixture until there are no white streaks. Pour the batter into the two prepared pans. Bake for 30 to 35 minutes, until a skewer inserted into the center comes out clean. Transfer to a wire rack to cool for 10 minutes. Remove from the pans and let cool completely.

For the Coconut Frosting: In a medium saucepan, beat the eggs, then stir in the sugar, evaporated milk, and butter. Cook, stirring, over medium heat about 10 to 12 minutes, until the mixture is thickened and bubbling. Add the coconut and pecans, stirring to combine. Set aside to cool completely. Place cake on a cake plate and spread coconut filling over the top. Place the remaining cake layer on top and finish spreading the cake with the remaining frosting.

Prep = 30 minutes **Cook** = 30 to 35 minutes **Yield** = 12 servings

Chocolate Graham Cake with Marshmallow Frosting

This is a simple cake with a grand presence. The frosting recipe yields a bowlful that is a bit too much for the cake, but is intended to be piled high for an impressive appearance. Excess frosting can be used to make cookie sandwiches or frost brownies. Bake the cake itself on a sheet pan, as the cake bakes up and over the sides of its pan, much as a muffin does. The sheet pan is added protection from overflow.

- 1½ cups (180 g) all-purpose flour
- ½ cup (45 g) unsweetened cocoa powder
- ½ cup (60 g) graham cracker crumbs
- 1 teaspoon baking powder
- ½ teaspoon baking soda
- ½ teaspoon salt
- 1 cup (2 sticks, or 225 g) unsalted butter, softened
- 1 cup (200 g) granulated sugar
- ½ cup (115 g) packed light brown sugar
- 2 large eggs
- 2 large egg yolks
- 1 teaspoon pure vanilla extract
- 1 cup (235 ml) buttermilk
- 4 ounces (115 g) bittersweet chocolate, melted and cooled
- ½ cup (50 g) crumbled graham crackers, for garnish

MARSHMALLOW FROSTING:
- 6 tablespoons (90 ml) water
- 1¼ cups (413 g) light corn syrup
- ¾ cup plus 1 tablespoon (163 g) granulated sugar
- 4 large egg whites
- Pinch of salt
- Pinch of cream of tartar
- 2 tablespoons (28 ml) vanilla extract

Preheat oven to 350°F (180°C, or gas mark 4). Butter and flour a 9-inch (22.5 cm) cake pan. In a mixing bowl, whisk together the flour, cocoa powder, graham cracker crumbs, baking powder, baking soda, and salt; set aside. In the bowl of a stand mixer fitted with the paddle attachment beat the butter with the sugar and brown sugar until creamy and smooth, about 4 minutes. Add the eggs one at a time, blending well after each addition. Add the egg yolks, vanilla, and melted chocolate and blend well. Add ½ cup (60 g) of the flour mixture, then ½ cup (120 ml) of the buttermilk; continue adding, alternating between the two, beginning and ending with the flour mixture. Pour the batter into the prepared pan and bake on the center rack of the oven for 60 to 70 minutes, until a skewer inserted in the center comes out clean. Transfer cake to a cooling rack and let cool for 30 minutes.

For Marshmallow Frosting: In a small saucepan fitted with a candy thermometer, bring the water, corn syrup, and ¾ cup (150 g) of sugar to 246°F (119°C).

In the meantime, in a clean, dry mixing bowl, with an electric mixer, beat the egg whites, salt, and cream of tartar until creamy and foamy, about 2 minutes. Still whisking, sprinkle in the remaining 1 tablespoon of sugar and continue to whisk until the whites hold very soft peaks, about 2 minutes. While mixing on slow speed, carefully drizzle in the hot syrup. Turn the mixer to high and whisk until thick, fluffy, and just warm, about 5 minutes. Turn the mixer to low and whisk in the vanilla.

Invert cake onto a plate and then invert right side up onto a cake plate. Frost with the Marshmallow Frosting, scatter graham cracker crumbs over the top, and serve.

Prep = 30 minutes **Cook** = 60 to 70 minutes **Yield** =

Cranberry-Mango Upside-Down Cake

I have met many cranberry upside-down cakes, but know none that combine the sweet tropical flavor of mango and the subtle, velvety smoothness of white chocolate. The white chocolate adds a creamy layer of flavor to this delicious cake. Dried, fresh, even frozen cranberries work in this recipe. If you don't use fresh or frozen berries, look for dried berries that are plump and tender, not overly dry and shriveled.

5	ounces (140 g) white chocolate, melted
1	cup (2 sticks, or 225 g) unsalted butter, at room temperature, divided
1	cup (200 g) granulated sugar
1	cup (150 g) plump dried or fresh cranberries
1/2	cup (44 g) chopped dried mango
1/4	cup (30 g) chopped pistachios
1	cup plus 2 tablespoons (135 g) all-purpose flour
1/2	cup (50 g) ground oats
1	teaspoon baking powder
1	teaspoon ground allspice
1/4	teaspoon salt
3	large eggs
1/3	cup (80 ml) whole milk
1	teaspoon vanilla extract

GLAZE:

1/2	cup (120 ml) cranberry juice
1	tablespoon (20 g) honey
1/2	cup (100 g) granulated sugar

Preheat oven to 350°F (180°C, or gas mark 4). Butter or spray with nonstick cooking spray an 8-inch (20 cm) cake pan. In the top of a double boiler, melt the white chocolate and set aside.

In a small saucepan over medium heat, melt 1 stick (112 g) of the butter with $\frac{1}{2}$ cup (100 g) of the sugar, stirring just until the sugar is dissolved. Pour the mixture into the cake pan, rotating the pan to evenly distribute the mixture. Sprinkle the cranberries in an even layer in the pan, top with mango in an even layer and then the pistachios, and set aside. In a mixing bowl, whisk together the flour, ground oats, baking powder, allspice, and salt. In the bowl of a stand mixer fitted with the paddle attachment, mix the remaining 1 stick (112 g) of butter with the remaining $\frac{1}{2}$ cup (100 g) of sugar until smooth. Add the eggs one at a time, blending well and scraping the sides of the bowl after each addition. Add half of the flour mixture and blend to combine. Add the white chocolate, milk, and vanilla and blend to combine. Scrape the sides of the bowl, add the remaining flour mixture, and blend just to combine. Place cake on the middle rack of oven and bake for 1 hour, or until a wooden skewer inserted into the center comes out almost clean. Remove from oven, run a sharp knife around edges to release, and invert cake onto a cake plate. Let cool for 5 minutes, then serve warm with the glaze.

Prepare the Glaze: In a small saucepan over medium-high heat, combine the cranberry juice with the honey and $\frac{1}{2}$ cup (100 g) sugar. Bring to a boil and cook for 2 minutes; remove from heat and set aside to cool for 5 minutes.

Prep = 20 minutes **Cook** = 1 hour **Chill** = 5 minutes
Yield =10 to 12 servings

Olive Oil–Madeira Cake

The richer the olive oil you choose, the more intense the flavor. A good rule of thumb is the darker the shade of green in the olive oil, the more robust it is.

3	cups (330 g) cake flour
2¹/₂	teaspoons baking powder
³/₄	teaspoons salt
1¹/₃	cups (267 g) granulated sugar
3	eggs
2	teaspoons finely grated orange zest
2	teaspoons finely grated lemon zest
¹/₂	teaspoon vanilla extract
¹/₄	teaspoon ground cardamom
²/₃	cup (160 ml) Madeira
¹/₂	cup (120 ml) milk
³/₄	cup (175 ml) olive oil
¹/₂	cup (58 g) chopped hazelnuts, toasted
¹/₂	cup (88 g) chopped white chocolate
	Confectioners' sugar for dusting

Preheat oven to 350°F (180°C, or gas mark 4). Butter bottom and sides of a 10-inch (25 cm) cake pan.

Sift together the flour, baking powder, and salt into a mixing bowl; set aside. In another large mixing bowl, whisk together the sugar, eggs, orange zest, lemon zest, vanilla extract, and cardamom until creamy. Add the Madeira, milk, and olive oil, whisking to combine. Gradually add the dry ingredients, thoroughly whisking. Add the hazelnuts and white chocolate; stir to incorporate. Scrape batter into cake pan, spreading evenly. Bake until a skewer inserted in the center of the cake comes out clean or with minimal crumbs, about 35 minutes. Remove the pan from oven and place on a rack to cool. Once cool, run a knife around the sides to loosen, invert cake onto a cake plate, and dust with confectioners' sugar.

To toast the hazelnuts: Preheat oven to 300°F (150°C, or gas mark 2). Spread hazelnuts in an even layer on an ungreased sheet pan. Place pan on center rack of the oven and bake for 12 to 15 minutes, until nuts begin to brown—do not overcook as the nuts will continue to toast when removed from the oven. Remove and set aside to cool.

Prep = 20 minutes **Cook** =35 minutes **Chill** =1 hour
Yield = 12 servings

Banana-Nut Cocoa Cake

This rich, dense chocolate cake embraces the flavor of ripened bananas. It takes a while to bake, but is worth the wait. When testing for doneness, a bit of the cake will still stick to the skewer but only as moist crumbs.

8	tablespoons (1 stick, or 112 g) unsalted butter
1/2	cup (45 g) unsweetened cocoa powder
3/4	cup (175 ml) water
1	cup (200 g) granulated sugar
1	cup (225 g) firmly packed light brown sugar
2	eggs plus 1 egg yolk
1/2	cup (120 ml) buttermilk
1	cup (225 g) mashed ripe bananas (about 2)
1/4	cup (61 g) applesauce
1	tablespoon (15 ml) vanilla extract
1	tablespoon (15 ml) dark rum
2	cups (240 g) all-purpose flour
1	teaspoon baking soda
1 1/2	teaspoons ground cinnamon
1/4	teaspoon salt
1	cup (110 g) chopped pecans

GLAZE:

8	ounces (225 g) semisweet chocolate, chopped
8	tablespoons (1 stick, or 112 g) butter or margarine
1/4	cup (60 ml) half-and-half
2	tablespoons (28 ml) dark rum
1	cup (110 g) chopped pecans

Preheat oven to 350°F (180°C, or gas mark 4). Oil and flour a 9-inch (22.5 cm) springform pan. In a medium saucepan, melt the butter over medium heat. Add the cocoa and whisk until well combined. Remove from the heat and whisk in the water. Meanwhile, using a stand mixer fitted with the paddle attachment, beat the sugars with the eggs and egg yolk until creamy—about 3 minutes—adding the eggs one at a time. Add the buttermilk and combine. Add the applesauce, bananas, vanilla, and rum. Beat until well combined. In a bowl, whisk together the flour, baking soda, salt, and cinnamon. Add one-third of the dry ingredients at a time to the wet mixture, blending well and scraping the sides of the mixing bowl after each addition. Add pecans and blend just to combine. Pour mixture into the prepared springform pan. Bake on middle shelf of oven for about 90 minutes, or until a skewer inserted into the center comes out mostly clean. Remove from oven and allow to cool for about 30 minutes. Remove the cake from pan and place on cake plate. Top with Glaze.

For the Glaze: Place the chocolate, butter, and half-and-half in the top of a double boiler, stirring to melt. Add the dark rum and pecans; stir to combine. Remove from heat and allow to cool for at least 15 minutes. The chocolate glaze may be used at this point, pouring over entire cake or onto individual slices. As the glaze cools it will change consistency, eventually becoming much like a frosting. You may choose which consistency you would prefer to use on the cake.

Prep = 20 minutes **Cook** = 90 minutes **Chill** = 30 minutes
Yield = 12 servings

Ultimate Chocolate Mocha Layer Cake

No book on chocolate would be complete without an "ultimate" chocolate cake. This one, layered high with chocolate, chocolate mocha, chocolate frosting, and gooey nuts, earns its title. It reigns as the ultimate cake of this book and maybe all of your cake recipes.

MOCHA FROSTING:
- 16 ounces (455 g) bittersweet chocolate, chopped
- 2 cups (475 ml) heavy cream
- 2 tablespoons (6 g) instant espresso powder
- 8 tablespoons (1 stick, or 112 g) unsalted butter, softened

CAKE:
- 2¾ cups (330 g) all-purpose flour
- ½ cup (45 g) unsweetened natural cocoa powder
- 2¼ teaspoons baking soda
- ½ teaspoon salt
- 1 cup (2 sticks, or 225 g) unsalted butter, softened
- 1 cup (225 g) packed dark brown sugar
- ¾ cup (150 g) granulated sugar
- 4 large eggs, at room temperature
- 4 ounces (115 g) unsweetened chocolate, melted and cooled
- 1 teaspoon vanilla extract
- 1½ cups (355 ml) buttermilk

GOOEY PECAN FILLING:
- 1 (12-ounce, or 340 g) can evaporated milk
- 1½ cups (300 g) granulated sugar
- 1 teaspoon instant espresso powder
- ¾ cup (1½ sticks, or 167 g) butter
- 4 egg yolks, slightly beaten
- 1½ teaspoons pure vanilla extract
- 2 cups (220 g) chopped pecans

COFFEE SYRUP:
- ½ cup (120 ml) strong brewed coffee
- ½ cup (100 g) granulated sugar
- ¼ cup (60 ml) Kahlúa coffee liqueur
- Chocolate shavings and chopped pecans, for garnish

(Continued on page 132)

(Continued from page 130)

For the Mocha Frosting: Melt the chocolate in the top of a double boiler. Remove from heat and set aside. In a small saucepan over medium heat, combine heavy cream with espresso powder and butter, until butter melts. Remove from heat and pour over the chocolate. Whisk. Allow to cool to a spreading consistency, about 30 minutes.

For the Cake: Place a rack in the center of the oven. Preheat to 350°F (180°C, or gas mark 4). Butter all sides of two 9 × 2-inch (22.5 × 5 cm) round cake pans. Line bottom of each with parchment paper; butter paper, and dust pans with flour, shaking out excess.

Sift the flour, cocoa powder, baking soda, and salt into a small bowl; set aside. Using a stand mixer fitted with the paddle attachment, beat the butter and sugars until light and fluffy, about 4 minutes. Add eggs one at a time, blending well. Add chocolate and vanilla; beat until just combined. Reduce speed to low, and add flour mixture in three batches, alternating with the buttermilk in two batches, beginning and ending with the flour. Blend after each addition. Scrape the sides of the bowl and mix again. Divide batter between the cake pans, spreading evenly. Bake until a wooden skewer inserted in the center of one cake comes out clean, 25 to 35 minutes. Transfer cakes to a cooling rack. Once completely cool, loosen sides of cakes with a knife and invert the cakes onto trays.

For the Gooey Pecan Filling: In a large saucepan over medium heat, stir together the milk, sugar, espresso powder, butter, egg yolks, and vanilla. Stirring constantly, cook until thick and golden brown about 12 minutes. Remove from the heat, stir in pecans, and set aside to cool.

For the Coffee Syrup: In a small saucepan over medium heat, stir together the coffee, sugar, and Kahlúa, heating until the sugar is dissolved; set aside to cool completely.

To build the cake: Trim the tops of each cake to create a flat surface. Halve each cake horizontally, using a long, serrated knife. Place one cake layer flat on a cake plate, inside facing up. Brush the cake with one-fourth of the Coffee Syrup. Spread with half of the Gooey Pecan Filling. Place second cake layer on top, brush with one-fourth of the Coffee Syrup; top with a layer of Mocha Frosting about ¼ inch (0.6 cm) thick. Top with third cake layer, brushing with one-fourth of the coffee syrup and topping with remaining pecan filling. Top with last cake layer, brush with remaining Coffee Syrup. Frost the entire cake top first and then working on the sides from the bottom of the cake up. Top cake with chocolate shavings and chopped pecans.

Prep = 45 minutes **Cook** = 35 minutes
Yield = 8 to 12 servings

Chocolate Marbled Sweet Potato Cheesecake with Coconut Streusel

My mother is a true Southern cook: She adds plenty of butter, flavor, and love to everything she makes. One of my favorite desserts is her Sweet Potato Cheesecake with toasted coconut. I have upped the ante by marbling the cheesecake with melted dark chocolate. I'm sure my mother won't mind.

CRUMB CRUST:

1½ cups (150 g) ground salted pretzels (ground to coarse crumbs)
½ cup (60 g) finely chopped pecans
¼ cup (18 g) flaked coconut
3 tablespoons (42 g) butter or margarine, melted

STREUSEL:

3 tablespoons (23 g) all-purpose flour
1 tablespoon (15 g) lightly packed light brown sugar
2 tablespoons (28 g) chilled butter, cut into small pieces
¼ cup (18 g) flaked coconut
¼ cup (28 g) pecan pieces

FILLING:

2 (8-ounce, or 225 g) packages cream cheese, softened
½ cup (115 g) firmly packed light brown sugar
½ cup (113 g) cooked, mashed sweet potato
¼ cup (60 ml) coffee liqueur (such as Kahlúa)
¼ teaspoon ground cinnamon
2 large eggs
4 ounces (115 g) dark chocolate, melted
Sweetened whipped cream for garnish
Ground cinnamon, for garnish

Preheat oven to 350°F (180°C, or gas mark 4). Lightly butter the bottom and sides of a 7-inch (17.5 cm) springform pan.

For Crumb Crust: Combine pretzels, chopped pecans, flaked coconut, and melted butter in a bowl, stirring well. Firmly press crumb mixture on bottom and 1 inch (2.5 cm) up the sides of prepared springform pan. Bake for 10 to 12 minutes, or until golden. Transfer to a rack to cool.

For Streusel: Reduce oven temperature to 325°F (170°C, or gas mark 3). In a mixing bowl, whisk together the flour and brown sugar. Cut in the chilled butter, using a pastry cutter, until the mixture resembles coarse corn meal. Add coconut and pecan pieces, and stir to combine; set aside.

For Filling: In a stand mixer fitted with the paddle attachment, beat the cream cheese with the brown sugar until smooth. Add sweet potato, Kahlúa, and cinnamon; beat on low until blended. Add eggs one at a time, beating well after each addition. Pour batter into prepared crust. Starting in the center and working outward toward the edges, begin to pour the melted chocolate in an even stream, forming rings. Using a skewer or dinner knife, working at four evenly spaced points around the cake, run the knife through the chocolate rings to make a marbled or webbed effect. Bake for 50 minutes. Remove, and sprinkle the top evenly with chilled streusel mixture. Return to the oven and bake for 25 minutes. Transfer to a wire rack and let cool to room temperature. Cover and chill. To serve, run a knife around the edges to loosen the cake from the pan; gently remove the pan sides. Top with whipped cream and cinnamon.

Prep = 30 minutes   **Cook** = 75 minutes   **Chill** = At least 3 hours
Yield = 1 (7-inch, or 17.5 cm) cheesecake

Chocolate Espresso Cake with Amaretto-Caramel Glaze

Rich and dense, this pound cake is a delight. Cocoa nibs add crunch and texture to each bite of the cake. If you omit them but want the crunch, try finely chopped pecans or walnuts.

1	cup (175 g) semisweet chocolate chips or squares, chopped
1	cup (175 g) chopped bittersweet chocolate with 70 percent cocoa
1	teaspoon vanilla extract
1/3	cup (80 ml) Amaretto
1	cup (235 ml) water
1/3	cup (30 g) unsweetened cocoa powder
1	tablespoon (3 g) instant espresso powder
2 1/2	cups (300 g) all-purpose flour
1/2	teaspoon baking soda
1/2	teaspoon ground cardamom
1	cup (2 sticks, or 225 g) butter, softened
2/3	cup (133 g) granulated sugar
2/3	cup (150 g) firmly packed brown sugar
4	eggs
1/2	cup (115 g) sour cream
1/2	cup (120 ml) whole milk
1/2	cup (50 g) cocoa nibs (optional)

AMARETTO GLAZE:

1/2	cup (100 g) granulated sugar
3	tablespoons (45 ml) water
2	tablespoons (30 ml) Amaretto
1/4	cup (30 g) slivered almonds
	Confectioners' sugar, to dust cake

Preheat oven to 300 °F (150°C, or gas mark 2). Prepare a tube pan by spraying thoroughly with nonstick cooking spray and then dust evenly with flour. In the top of a double boiler, melt the chocolate together; remove from heat and stir in the vanilla extract and Amaretto, then set aside to cool. In a small saucepan over high heat, bring 1 cup (235 ml) of water to a boil, add the cocoa powder and espresso powder, stirring until dissolved; set aside to cool. In a medium mixing bowl, sift together the flour, baking soda, and cardamom; set aside. In the bowl of a stand mixer fitted with the paddle attachment, cream the butter and sugars together on medium-high speed until smooth, about 3 minutes. Scrape the sides of the mixing bowl. Add the eggs one at a time, mixing in thoroughly after each addition. Add the sour cream and milk, ½ cup (120 ml) at a time, mixing well. Add the dry ingredients to the sugar mixture alternating with the espresso water, scraping the sides of the bowl and mixing in thoroughly with each addition, beginning and ending with the flour mixture. Blend on low speed until combined; fold in the cocoa nibs. Scrape the batter into the pan and smooth the top. Place the cake on the middle rack of the preheated oven and bake for 90 minutes, or until a wooden skewer inserted in the middle comes out clean.

For the Amaretto Glaze: In a small saucepan over medium-high heat, stir the sugar, water, and Amaretto; bring to a boil, cooking without stirring until an amber color and sugar is melted, about 5 minutes. Remove from heat, stir in the almonds, and set aside on a cooling rack for 5 minutes. Once cake is baked, remove from oven and let cool in the pan 10 minutes on a wire rack. Invert a cake plate on top of the tube pan and invert the pan, removing the cake pan carefully. Glaze cake with Amaretto Glaze, dust with confectioners' sugar, and serve.

Prep = 30 minutes   **Cook** = 90 minutes   **Yield** = 12 Servings

White Chocolate-Orange Ricotta Cheesecake

Cheesecake is an icon of indulgence; this one is no exception. Try ricotta cheese, for its moist, airy quality.

GRAHAM CRACKER CRUST:
- 1¼ cups (125 g) pecans
- ¼ cup (50 g) granulated sugar
- ½ cup (60 g) graham cracker crumbs
- 5 tablespoons (70 g) unsalted butter, melted

FILLING:
- 8 ounces (225 g) cream cheese, softened
- 7 ounces (200 g) whole-milk ricotta cheese
- Zest of 1 orange
- 1 cup (200 g) granulated sugar
- 1 teaspoon pure vanilla extract
- 4 eggs, separated
- ⅔ cup (160 ml) heavy cream
- 4 ounces (115 g) white chocolate chips or squares, melted

Preheat oven to 350°F (180°C, or gas mark 4). In the bowl of a food processor, finely grind the pecans. In a large mixing bowl, stir the pecans, sugar, graham cracker crumbs, and butter until well coated. Press into the bottom and halfway up the sides of a 9-inch (22.5 cm) springform pan. Place the pan on the middle rack of the oven and bake for 20 minutes. Remove from the oven and set aside to cool.

For the Filling: In a food processor, combine the cream cheese, ricotta cheese, orange zest, sugar, and vanilla. Blend until creamy, about 1 minute. Add the egg yolks and heavy cream and pulse to combine. In a medium mixing bowl, whisk the egg whites until soft peaks form. Gradually pour in the cream cheese mixture, folding into the egg whites with a rubber spatula. Pour the melted chocolate into the mixture and fold in, using the rubber spatula. Pour the mixture into the crust. Place on center rack of oven and bake for 1 hour or until set, until a wooden skewer inserted into the center comes out clean. Remove from the oven and let cool for 30 minutes. Remove the sides of pan and allow cake to cool completely.

Prep = 30 minutes **Cook** = 1 hour **Chill** = 1 hour
Yield = 12 servings

Chocolate Applesauce Cake

With warm spices and chocolate paired with the apples and sour cream, this cake is suitable for any occasion. Serve this cake as a dessert with whipped cream and a sprinkle of cinnamon or toast slices and serve with jam.

- 2½ cups (300 g) all-purpose flour
- ¼ cup (23 g) unsweetened cocoa powder
- 2 teaspoons baking powder
- 1 teaspoon baking soda
- 1 teaspoon ground ginger
- 1 teaspoon ground cinnamon
- 1 cup (2 sticks, 225 g) unsalted butter, softened
- 1 cup (225 g) lightly packed light brown sugar
- 3 large eggs
- 1 teaspoon pure vanilla extract
- ½ cup (115 g) sour cream
- ½ cup (123 g) applesauce
- 1 cup (175 g) chopped dark chocolate, melted and cooled
  Confectioners' sugar, for dusting

Preheat oven to 350°F (180°C, or gas mark 4). Butter and flour a tube pan. In a large mixing bowl, whisk together the flour, cocoa, baking powder, baking soda, ginger, and cinnamon; set aside. In the bowl of a stand mixer fitted with the paddle attachment, beat the butter with the brown sugar until creamy and smooth, about 5 minutes. Add the eggs one at a time, beating well after each addition. Add the vanilla, sour cream, and applesauce, beating just to combine. With the mixer running on low speed, add the melted chocolate in a steady stream to incorporate. Add the flour mixture 1 cup (120 g) at a time, blending well after each addition. Pour the batter into the tube pan. Bake on middle rack of the oven for 40 to 45 minutes, or until a wooden skewer inserted into the center comes out clean. Allow cake to cool in the pan on a wire rack for 10 minutes, then turn out onto a rack to cool completely. Dust with confectioners' sugar and serve.

Prep = 20 minutes **Cook** = 40 to 45 minutes **Chill** = 30 minutes
Yield = 12 servings

Cherry–Chocolate Pudding Cake

The cake cooks on top and a luscious cherry pudding cooks on the bottom—it is pure baking alchemy. Serve spoonfuls of this delight topped with whipped cream or vanilla ice cream.

   8 tablespoons (1 stick, or 112 g) butter, diced
   6 ounces (170 g) dark chocolate, chopped
   3 eggs, slightly beaten
   1 cup (200 g) granulated sugar
1½ teaspoons pure vanilla extract
1½ cups (180 g) all-purpose flour
   2 teaspoons baking powder
 ¾ cup (68 g) unsweetened cocoa powder
 ½ cup (120 ml) whole milk
   1 tablespoon (15 ml) orange liqueur
   1 cup (235 ml) jarred Morello cherries, drained
 ½ cup (115 g) brown sugar
   1 cup (235 ml) boiling water

Preheat oven to 350°F (180°C, or gas mark 4). Spray an 8-inch (20 cm) baking dish with nonstick cooking spray. Melt the butter with the chocolate in a saucepan over medium heat, stirring until smooth. In a mixing bowl, whisk the eggs with the sugar and vanilla. Gradually, in a steady stream, add the melted chocolate, stirring constantly to incorporate. In a separate mixing bowl, whisk together the flour, baking powder, and cocoa powder. Add to the chocolate mixture, stirring to combine. Add the milk, orange liqueur, and cherries, stirring to combine. Pour batter into baking dish. Combine brown sugar and cocoa powder in a mixing bowl. Pour boiling water over cocoa mixture, stirring until cocoa and sugar are dissolved. Pour mixture over batter. Gently place dish on center rack of oven and bake for 35 to 40 minutes. Remove and serve.

Prep = 20 minutes **Cook** =35 to 40 minutes
Yield = 8 servings

White Chocolate Ginger-Almond Cake

This is a deceptively simple cake with layers of flavor. Mild, virgin olive oil imparts an elegant, unexpected flavor to the cake. If you don't have olive oil, simply melt 6 tablespoons (83 g) butter with the chocolate instead. I have included three variations for presentation as this cake is quite versatile and can make a simple sheet cake or beautiful individual cakes.

1¼   cups (219 g) chopped white chocolate
¾   cup (175 ml) mild olive oil
½   cup (60 g) all-purpose flour
¼   cup (35 g) fine yellow cornmeal
1   cup (95 g) ground almonds
1   teaspoon ground ginger
4   large eggs, separated
1   teaspoon pure vanilla extract
¾   cup (150 g) granulated sugar
¼   teaspoon cream of tartar

WHITE CHOCOLATE GLAZE (page 222)

⅓   cup (42 g) chopped almonds, toasted

Preheat the oven to 350°F (180°C, or gas mark 4). Spray the bottom and sides of a 9 × 13-inch (22.5 × 32.5 cm) cake pan with nonstick cooking spray. Line the pan with parchment paper, letting it hang over the sides of the pan to allow for easy removal. In the top of a double boiler, melt the chocolate with the olive oil until smooth; set aside to cool slightly. In a small bowl, whisk together the flour, cornmeal, ground almonds, and ground ginger. In the bowl of a stand mixer fitted with the paddle attachment, beat the egg yolks and vanilla with ½ cup of the sugar (100 g) until thickened and pale, about 2 minutes. Add the melted chocolate and the flour mixture, beating just until combined. In a clean mixing bowl, whip the egg whites with the remaining ¼ cup (50 g) of sugar and cream of tartar until stiff peaks form, about 3 minutes. Using a rubber spatula, gently fold the egg whites into the chocolate mixture until just combined.

Pour the mixture into the prepared baking dish and bake for 30 minutes, or until a wooden skewer inserted in the center comes out clean. Allow to cool in pan on a cooling rack. Remove from the pan and cut into squares. Drizzle with glaze, sprinkle with toasted chopped almonds, and serve. For a more impressive presentation, using a 3-inch (7.6 cm) circle cutter, cut out six individual cakes, place on a wire rack, and coat with White Chocolate Glaze, letting it run over the sides. Let chocolate set and serve sprinkled with toasted chopped almonds. For individual layer cakes, cut eight circles with a 2½-inch (6.3 cm) circle cutter. Place four cakes on wire rack, spread with raspberry jam or prepared lemon curd. Place remaining four cakes on top, then pour white chocolate glaze over each cake, allowing to run over the sides randomly. Let glaze set and then serve sprinkled with toasted almonds. If using the circle cutters, reserve the excess cake to crumble over ice cream, in a trifle, over a mousse, or inside the Blueberry Chocolate Turnovers on page 70.

Prep = 20 minutes **Cook** =30 minutes **Chill** =1 hour
Yield = 16 squares or 6 individual 3-inch (7.5 cm) cakes
or 4 individual layer cakes

White Chocolate Raspberry Cheesecake with Almond Crust

Cheesecake is like ice cream: There are endless combinations of flavors and no limit to what you can put in them on them and around them. Here I have combined the subtlety of orange, the tartness of raspberries, and the richness of white chocolate.

ALMOND CRUST:

- 1 cup (120 g) graham cracker crumbs
- ½ cup (50 g) ground rolled oats
- 1 cup (95 g) ground almonds
- ⅓ cup (75 g) lightly packed light brown sugar
- 10 tablespoons (140 g) unsalted butter or margarine, melted

FILLING:

- 4 cups (1 kg) cream cheese, softened
- 1 cup (200 g) granulated sugar
- 1 teaspoon orange extract
- Zest of 1 orange
- ⅔ cup (160 ml) whole milk
- 3½ cups (613 g) chopped white chocolate, melted and cooled
- 5 large eggs, beaten
- 2 cups (250 g) fresh raspberries
- White Chocolate Curls (page 220)

Preheat oven to 350°F (180°C, or gas mark 4). Butter a 10-inch (25 cm) springform pan.

For the Almond Crust: Combine the graham cracker crumbs, ground oats, ground almonds, brown sugar, and butter in a bowl, stirring to combine well. Firmly press into the bottom and up the sides of the prepared springform pan. Bake for 10 minutes, set aside.

Prep = 30 minutes **Cook** = 50 to 60 minutes **Yield** = 12 servings

Decrease oven temperature to 325°F (170°C, or gas mark 3).

For the Filling: In a stand mixer fitted with the paddle attachment, beat the cream cheese, sugar, orange extract, and zest until creamy. Add the milk and melted chocolate, beating just to combine. Add the eggs, beating on low to combine; increase speed and beat until smooth. Pour the mixture into the cooked crust, scatter raspberries evenly over the top, and bake for 50 to 60 minutes—the filling will be a bit jiggly in the middle. Turn off the heat, open the oven door slightly, and allow cake to cool in the oven. Chill for at least 2 hours or overnight in the refrigerator. Before serving, garnish with White Chocolate Curls.

Black and White Chocolate Velvet Pound Cake

This marbled pound cake plays with the subtle flavor of white chocolate and the richness of a fine dark chocolate, enhancing the classic.

1³/₄ cups (210 g) all-purpose flour
¼ cup (23 g) unsweetened cocoa powder
1 teaspoon baking powder
¼ teaspoon salt
1 cup (2 sticks, or 225 g) unsalted butter, at room temperature
1 cup (200 g) sugar
4 large eggs, at room temperature
1 teaspoon vanilla extract
1 teaspoon almond extract
4 ounces (115 g) unsweetened chocolate, melted
4 ounces (115 g) white chocolate, melted

Center a rack in the oven and preheat to 325°F (170°C, or gas mark 3). Butter a 9 × 5-inch (22.5 × 13 cm) loaf pan and place on a sheet pan. Whisk the flour, cocoa, baking powder, and salt together in a medium bowl; set aside. Working with a stand mixer fitted with the paddle attachment, beat the butter and sugar on high speed until pale and fluffy, about 5 minutes. Scrape down the bowl and beater and reduce the speed to medium. Add the eggs one at a time, beating for 2 minutes between each addition. Scrape down the bowl and beater often while mixing. Add the vanilla and almond extracts and blend. Reduce speed to low and add the flour mixture, beating just to incorporate. Scrape half of the batter into a bowl, and half into another. In one bowl, stir in the unsweetened chocolate until well combined. In the other bowl, add the white chocolate, stirring to combine. Alternately spoon the two batters into the prepared loaf pan, then run a knife in a zigzag formation through the batters to marble them.

Bake until a wooden skewer inserted into the center comes out clean, about 75 minutes. Remove the from oven and let cool on a rack for 30 minutes. Run a knife along the edges of the pan and turn the cake onto cooling rack and allow to cool completely.

Prep = 20 minutes **Cook** = 75 minutes
Yield = 6 to 10 Servings

White Chocolate-Orange Pound Cake

This classic cake is scented with orange extract. Consider substituting lemon extract and zest for the orange extract and zest.

- 1½ cups (180 g) all-purpose flour, plus extra for dusting
- ½ teaspoon baking soda
- ¼ teaspoon salt
- 12 tablespoons (1 ½ sticks, or 167 g) unsalted butter, at room temperature
- 1 cup (200 g) granulated sugar
- 1 tablespoon (20 g) honey
- 1 teaspoon vanilla extract
- ¾ teaspoon orange extract
- 1 teaspoon orange zest
- 2 large eggs, at room temperature
- 4 ounces (115 g) white chocolate chips or squares, chopped
- ½ cup (115 g) sour cream, at room temperature

Preheat oven to 325°F (170°C, or gas mark 3). Lightly grease an 8 × 4-inch (20 × 10 cm) loaf pan and dust with flour. In a bowl, whisk the flour, baking soda, and salt until blended; set aside. In another bowl, using a mixer on medium-high speed, beat the butter, sugar, honey, vanilla extract, orange extract, and orange zest until light and fluffy, about 3 minutes. Add the eggs one at a time, beating well after each addition, until just blended. In the top of a double boiler, melt the white chocolate. Slowly drizzle the still-warm chocolate into the egg mixture on low speed until well combined. Add half of the dry ingredients and blend on low until just incorporated. Add the sour cream and remaining dry ingredients; blend until just combined. Scrape sides of the bowl and beaters once or twice while mixing.

Scrape the batter into the prepared pan, tapping gently to even out the batter. Bake the cake on the center rack of the oven until a wooden skewer inserted in the center comes out clean, about 80 minutes. Transfer to a rack and let cool for 15 minutes.

Run a knife around the inside of the pan to loosen the sides, invert the cake out of the pans and lay it on its side to continue to cool. Serve warm or at room temperature.

Prep = 20 minutes **Cook** = 80 minutes **Chill** = 1 hour
Yield = 10 servings

Chocolate Polenta Cake with Chocolate-Orange Ganache

Polenta cake, a classic Italian dessert, is dense but moist, with the toothsome texture of fine cornmeal. I added chocolate, enriching the flavor further by topping it with an orange-scented ganache. Ground pine nuts provide robust nuttiness for added depth.

1	cup (140 g)	polenta or finely ground yellow cornmeal
½	cup (60 g)	all-purpose flour
⅓	cup (30 g)	unsweetened cocoa powder
2½	teaspoons	baking powder
1	cup (125 g)	ground pine nuts
1	cup (2 sticks, or 225 g)	unsalted butter, softened
1	cup (200 g)	granulated sugar
3	whole eggs	
6	egg yolks	
½	teaspoon	almond extract
1	teaspoon	pure vanilla extract
½	cup (120 ml)	whole milk

CHOCOLATE GANACHE:

¾	cup (175 ml)	heavy cream
6	ounces (170 g)	bittersweet chocolate, chopped
1	teaspoon	orange zest
½	teaspoon	orange extract
⅛	teaspoon	ground nutmeg

Preheat oven to 350°F (180°C, or gas mark 4). Butter the sides and bottom of a 9-inch (22.5 cm) springform pan, add a disk of parchment paper to the bottom, and butter it. In a mixing bowl, whisk together the polenta, flour, cocoa powder, baking powder, and ground pine nuts; set aside. In the bowl of a stand mixer fitted with the paddle attachment, beat together the butter and sugar until creamy and smooth, about 3 minutes. Add the eggs one at a time, blending well after each addition. Add the egg yolks and almond and vanilla extracts, blending on low to combine. Add the flour mixture in two separate batches, adding the milk in between, blending on low just to combine after each addition. Pour the batter into the prepared pan. Bake for 40 minutes, or until the cake starts to pull away from the sides of the pan and a wooden skewer inserted in the center comes out clean. Transfer the pan to a rack and let cool for 10 to 15 minutes. Remove the springform sides and invert the cake onto a plate, remove the bottom and parchment, and invert back to a cake plate. Serve drenched with the chocolate ganache.

To prepare the Chocolate Ganache: In a saucepan over medium heat, warm the cream just until steam rises and bubbles form around the edges. Pour the cream over the chocolate in a bowl, let stand for 2 minutes, then stir until smooth. Add the orange zest, extract, and nutmeg, stirring to combine. Let cool to desired consistency, pour over the cake, and serve.

Prep = 20 minutes **Cook** = 40 minutes **Chill** = 10 to 15 minutes
Yield = 10 servings

Chocolate-Orange Yogurt Cake

This classic French yogurt cake pairs bright citrus of oranges with almonds. While optional, the orange marmalade sauce is suitable for any number of treats.

- ³⁄₄ cup (90 g) all-purpose flour
- ¼ cup (23 g) unsweetened cocoa powder
- ½ cup (50 g) ground almonds
- 2 teaspoons baking powder
- ⅛ teaspoon salt
- ½ cup (100 g) granulated sugar
- ½ cup (115 g) lightly packed dark brown sugar
- 1 teaspoon orange zest
- ½ cup (125 g) plain yogurt
- 3 large eggs
- ¼ teaspoon pure vanilla extract
- ½ teaspoon orange extract, optional
- ½ cup (120 ml) canola oil
- Confectioners' sugar, for dusting

SAUCE:
- ½ cup (160 g) orange marmalade
- 2 tablespoons (28 ml) water

Preheat oven to 350°F (180°C, or gas mark 4). Grease or spray an 8-inch (20 cm) round cake pan with nonstick cooking spray. In a mixing bowl, whisk together the first five ingredients. In another bowl, whisk together sugars, orange zest, yogurt, eggs, vanilla, orange extract, and oil until combined and smooth. Add the wet ingredients to the dry, mixing with a wooden spoon to combine. Pour the batter into the prepared pan and bake for 30 minutes, or until a wooden skewer inserted into the center comes out clean. Transfer the pan to a rack and let cool for 5 minutes. Run a knife along the edge to loosen the cake from the pan, invert onto a plate, and invert again onto a cake plate to cool completely. Dust with confectioners' sugar and serve.

Prepare the Sauce: Melt the orange marmalade with the water in a small saucepan over medium heat. Drizzle a dessert plate with sauce and serve a slice of cake on top.

Prep = 15 minutes   **Cook** = 30 minutes   **Chill** = 30 minutes
Yield = 10 to 12 servings

5

Unexpected Chocolate Savory Sensations

Infused Grating Chocolates

I was grating chocolate into my chili one night and thought, "What if this chocolate was flavored with something to add even more depth to the dish?" Thus, my infused grating chocolates were born. Many premium chocolate bars are already infused with unique flavors and they can be used in this same fashion. These are so simple and inexpensive to make, you will want to keep them on hand as finishing flavors for many meat, poultry, seafood, and pasta dishes. To mold them, I use a ramekin, but if you're hosting a special dinner party, use a beautiful candy mold to shape your grating chocolate for a truly unique and elegant touch.

ANCHO CHILE GRATING CHOCOLATE

4	ounces (115 g) premium dark chocolate, melted
1/4	teaspoon ancho chili powder
1/4	teaspoon grated lime zest
1	tablespoon (6 g) cocoa nibs

Line a 5-ounce (150 ml) ramekin or dish with plastic wrap large enough to come up the sides and leave an overhang of at least 1 inch (2.5 cm), pressing well against the sides and bottom to get full coverage. In the top of a double boiler, melt the chocolate over boiling water. Remove chocolate from the heat and add the chili powder, lime zest, and cocoa nibs, stirring to combine. Pour the chocolate into the prepared dish. Set aside to cool and harden completely. To unmold, pull the plastic up and out of the dish, then peel the plastic away from the chocolate. Use the chocolate to grate over salads, meats, poultry, and pasta as a finishing flavor. Keep the chocolate covered in a cool, dry place for up to 3 months.

THREE-PEPPER GRATING CHOCOLATE

- 4 ounces (115 g) premium dark chocolate, chopped
- 2 ounces (55 g) premium milk chocolate, chopped
- 1 teaspoon black peppercorns
- ½ teaspoon green peppercorns or pink peppercorns
- Pinch of ground white pepper

Line a 5-ounce (150 ml) ramekin or dish with plastic wrap large enough to come up the sides and leave an overhang of at least 1 inch (2.5 cm), pressing well against the sides and bottom to get full coverage. In a mortar and pestle, grind the peppercorns together. In the top of a double boiler, melt the chocolate over boiling water. Remove the chocolate from heat and add the peppers, stirring to combine. Pour the chocolate into the prepared dish. Set aside to cool and harden completely. To unmold, pull the plastic up and out of the dish, then peel the plastic away from the chocolate. Use the chocolate to grate over salads, meats, poultry, and pasta as a finishing flavor. Keep the chocolate covered in a cool, dry place for up to 3 months.

GINGER GRATING CHOCOLATE

- 6 ounces (170 g) premium dark chocolate, chopped
- 1 teaspoon finely minced crystallized ginger
- ½ teaspoon dried green tea leaves
- Dash ground cardamom

Line a 5-ounce (150 ml) ramekin or dish with plastic wrap large enough to come up the sides and leave an overhang of at least 1 inch (2.5 cm), pressing well against the sides and bottom to get full coverage. In the top of a double boiler, melt the chocolate over boiling water. Remove the chocolate from heat and add the remaining ingredients, stirring to combine. Pour the chocolate into the prepared dish. Set aside to cool and harden completely. To unmold, pull the plastic up and out of dish, then peel the plastic away from the chocolate. Use the chocolate to grate over salads, meats, poultry, and pasta as a finishing flavor. Keep the chocolate covered in a cool, dry place for up to 3 months.

Compound Butters

Compound butters are used in restaurants as a simple finishing sauce or flavoring. Usually a combination of herbs and spices are mixed into softened butter, which is then rechilled and sliced. Compound butters are an easy way to add flavor to any meal. Use these unique butters only as toppings or spreads on breads; do not use them for cooking, as the chocolate in them will burn in the skillet.

FOR ALL BUTTER RECIPES: In a small mixing bowl combine all the ingredients. Using a fork, mash the ingredients together to combine. Scrape out the mixture onto a piece of plastic wrap, forming a 6-inch (15 cm) cylinder. Roll up the cylinder in plastic wrap to cover. Place in the freezer and allow to harden for at least 1 hour. To use, simply cut slices and place on grilled meats, fish, or poultry.

WHITE CHOCOLATE AND WHITE PEPPER

- 8 tablespoons (1 stick, or 112 g) unsalted butter, softened
- 1 ounce (28 g) premium quality white chocolate, melted
- 1/4 teaspoon ground white pepper
- 1/4 teaspoon sea salt

CRANBERRY SAGE WITH WHITE CHOCOLATE

- 8 tablespoons (1 stick, or 112 g) butter or margarine, softened
- 1 tablespoon (9 g) finely minced dried cranberries
- 1/4 teaspoon finely minced fresh sage, or 1/8 teaspoon dried rubbed
- 1 ounce (28 g) premium quality white chocolate, melted

ORANGE CHOCOLATE

- 8 tablespoons (1 stick, or 112 g) butter or margarine, softened
- 1/2 teaspoon grated orange zest
- 1/4 teaspoons orange extract
- 1 ounce (28 g) premium dark chocolate, melted

Spiced Nuts with Cocoa Nibs and Chocolate Chips

Rosemary, garlic, and chocolate: What at first feels counterintuitive, tastes divine. You can vary the proportions of types of nuts you use according to your preferences.

2   cups (200 g) pecan halves
1   cup (130 g) cashews
1   cup (145 g) almonds
1   cup (110 g) walnuts
1   tablespoon (15 ml) olive oil
2   shallots, sliced thinly into rings
3   cloves garlic, sliced thinly
2   tablespoons (28 g) unsalted butter
¼   cup (8 g) chopped fresh rosemary
½   teaspoon chili powder
1   tablespoon (15 g) firmly packed light brown sugar
1   tablespoon (6 g) coarsely ground sea salt
1   cup (175 g) semisweet chocolate chips
½   cup (50 g) cocoa nibs

Preheat the oven to 350°F (180°C, or gas mark 4). Toss the nuts in a large mixing bowl to combine. Transfer nuts to a sheet pan, spreading in a single layer. Bake for 10 to 12 minutes, until nuts are toasted and fragrant. Transfer the nuts back to the mixing bowl and set aside. Heat the olive oil in small skillet over medium heat. Add the shallots and garlic, cooking until golden, about 4 minutes. Transfer to a paper towel to drain. Melt the butter and pour it over the nuts; add the rosemary, chili powder, brown sugar, and salt and stir to combine. Toss in the shallots and garlic, then add the chocolate chips and cocoa nibs, stirring to combine. Serve immediately.

Prep = 20 minutes   **Cook** = 12 minutes   **Cool** = 20 minutes
Yield = About 6 cups

Chocolate Chip Snack Mix

When I host small parties, I am always looking for a snack mix to manage everyone's appetite. This is a great combination of flavors. A little salty, a bit crunchy, and plenty sweet, with a hint of chocolate—you can't go wrong.

½ tablespoon unsalted butter
1 cup (130 g) salted almonds
½ cup (88 g) semisweet chocolate chips
½ cup (88 g) milk chocolate chips
½ cup (115 g) salted sunflower seeds
½ cup (75 g) dried cranberries
½ cup (75 g) golden raisins
2 cups (250 g) garlic rye chips
1 cup (125 g) sesame sticks
1 cup (100 g) dried banana chips

Preheat oven to 350°F (180°C, or gas mark 4). Melt the butter in a baking dish in the oven. Add the nuts, tossing to coat, and bake for 7 minutes, or until lightly toasted. Remove from the oven, and let cool. Add the remaining ingredients, tossing to combine. Store in an airtight container for up to one week.

Prep = 10 minutes **Cook** = 7 minutes **Cook** = 30 minutes
Yield = About 8 cups

Chocolate Barbecue Sauce

I use barbecue sauce a lot for quick marinades and flavorings. Whether on chicken, pork, or in hamburgers, barbecue sauce punches up many quick meals. Keep this one on hand rather than a bottle of a store-bought brand. The chocolate, as it does in chilies and stews, adds a depth of flavor—you can always add more chocolate, if you prefer.

1/4	cup (60 ml) canola oil
2	yellow onions, diced finely
4	garlic cloves, minced
1	(12-ounce, or 355 ml) bottle dark ale
1/2	cup (120 ml) cider vinegar
2	tablespoons (28 ml) Worcestershire sauce
1	cup (225 g) ketchup
1/2	cup (115 g) firmly packed light brown sugar
1/4	cup (85 g) molasses
1/4	cup (63 g) Dijon mustard
1/2	teaspoon red pepper flakes
1	tablespoon (7 g) paprika
1/4	cup (44 g) chopped dark chocolate
1	teaspoon salt
2	teaspoons freshly ground black pepper

In a medium saucepan heat the oil over medium-high heat. Add the onions and sauté until translucent and tender, about 3 minutes. Add the garlic and cook for 2 minutes, being careful not to let it brown. Add the remaining ingredients, stirring to combine. Bring to a slow boil, reduce the heat to a low simmer, and cook for 5 minutes. Remove from the heat and allow to cool completely before placing in a jar with a tight-fitting lid. Store refrigerated for up to 2 weeks.

Prep = 20 minutes **Cook** = 10 minutes **Yield** = About 4 cups (945 ml)

Chocolate Cherry Port Sauce

This classic sweet sauce discovered its savory side in this recipe. The chocolate, port, and cherries are perfect for a well-grilled steak or chicken. Softening the dried cherries in the port takes some time, but the time is worth it—the cherries soak up the port and become plump and juicy for the sauce. Make ahead of time and cover; reheat before serving.

- $^3/_4$ cup (180 ml) good-quality tawny port
- $^1/_2$ cup (75 g) dried cherries
- 2 tablespoons (28 ml) olive oil
- 1 large shallot, minced
- 1 tablespoon (15 ml) sherry vinegar
- $^1/_2$ cup (120 ml) chicken stock
- 2 ounces (55 g) dark chocolate, chopped
- 2 tablespoons (28 g) butter, chilled
- Salt and black pepper

In a small bowl, pour the $^1/_2$ cup (120 ml) of the port over the cherries to cover. Let macerate for at least 30 minutes, or up to overnight. In a saucepan, heat the olive oil over medium-high heat. Add the shallot and sauté until tender, about 2 minutes. Add the macerated cherries with the port and heat through. Add the additional $^1/_4$ cup (60 ml) of port, vinegar, and chicken stock. Bring to a boil and let reduce for 5 minutes. Add the chocolate, stirring constantly until melted. Remove from heat, stir in butter, and season to taste with salt and black pepper. Serve warm over steak or chicken.

Prep = 30 minutes **Cook** = 10 minutes **Yield** = About 2 cups ( )

Pear and Walnut Salad

Poached pears and this cocoa-infused pomegranate vinaigrette are perfect complements.

- 1 cup (235 ml) red wine
- 2 cups (475 ml) apple juice
- 1/2 cup (120 ml) pomegranate juice
- 1 cup (235 ml) water
- 1/2 cup (100 g) granulated sugar
- 1 stick cinnamon
- 2 whole cloves
- 4 black peppercorns
- 2 Anjou pears, peeled

VINAIGRETTE:
- 1/4 cup (60 ml) balsamic vinegar
- 1/4 cup (60 ml) pomegranate juice
- 2 teaspoons unsweetened cocoa powder
- 1/2 teaspoon granulated sugar
- 1/2 teaspoon lemon zest
- 2 tablespoons (30 ml) lemon juice
- 1 tablespoon (4 g) chopped fresh tarragon
- 1 tablespoon (4 g) chopped fresh flat leaf parsley
- 1/3 cup (80 ml) extra-virgin olive oil

- 1 teaspoon cocoa nibs
- 4 cups (80 g) salad greens
- 1/2 cup (60 g) chopped walnuts, toasted
- 1/3 cup (40 g) crumbled goat cheese

Place the red wine, apple juice, pomegranate juice, water, sugar, cinnamon, cloves, and peppercorns in a large saucepan. Bring to a boil, add the pears, and poach for 20 minutes, until tender but still firm. Remove from the poaching liquid and set aside to cool. Once cool, cut into quarters and remove the seeds. Slice the pears thinly.

To make the Vinaigrette: Place all ingredients in a jar and shake vigorously until combined. Refrigerate until ready to use. To serve, toss salad greens with vinaigrette and place on four plates. Top with sliced pears, toasted walnuts, and crumbled goat cheese.

Prep = 15 minutes **Cook** = 20 minutes
Yield = 4 servings

Baked Black Beans with Chocolate

These baked beans are rich and flavorful—a true barbecue favorite. The addition of the chocolate at the end of cooking serves to round out the flavors. Bacon, molasses, and cider vinegar are just a few of the ingredients that pack this dish with great taste.

2 cups (450 g) dried black beans
1 tablespoon (15 ml) olive oil
6 slices bacon, chopped
1 sweet yellow onion, diced
3 cloves garlic, minced
1 jalapeño, cleaned and minced
½ cup (115 g) firmly packed light brown sugar
2 tablespoons (40 g) dark molasses
2 teaspoons ground cumin
2 teaspoons chili powder
1 teaspoon dried oregano
2 tablespoons (28 ml) apple cider vinegar
  Freshly ground black pepper and salt
2 ounces (55 g) dark chocolate

Cook beans according to package instructions. Once cooked through, drain the beans, reserving 2½ cups (570 ml) of cooking liquid, and set aside. In a large Dutch oven, heat the olive oil over medium-high heat. Add the chopped bacon, cooking until crisp. Remove the bacon, leaving behind the grease. Add the onion to the pan, cooking for 3 minutes, until tender. Add the garlic and jalapeño and cook for 2 minutes. Add the brown sugar, molasses, cumin, chili powder, oregano, and cider vinegar; stir in the bacon. Add the drained beans and reserved cooking liquid. Bring to a boil and reduce the heat to a simmer; cover and cook over low heat for 1 hour. Partially remove the cover and cook for an additional 30 minutes. Season to taste with salt and pepper; stir in chocolate until melted. Serve warm.

Prep = 20 minutes **Cook** = 1½ hours **Yield** = 8 servings

Salad of Asiago Pepper Crisps with Cocoa Nibs and Beets

Asiago cheese was chosen for its melting properties: At high temperatures, it melts but keeps its form rather than turning to liquid. These cups are as easy to make as they are impressive to serve, not to mention flavorful. Once all the salad components are ready, it is assembled quickly. You can make several Asiago cups at a time and stack them with paper towels layered between them for up to three days.

ASIAGO CUPS:
- 1½ cups (120 g) shredded Asiago cheese
- 2 tablespoons (12 g) cocoa nibs
- ¾ teaspoon coarsely ground black pepper

COCOA BALSAMIC DRESSING:
- ¼ cup (60 ml) balsamic vinegar
- 1½ teaspoons unsweetened cocoa powder
- ½ teaspoon granulated sugar
- ½ teaspoon orange zest
- 2 tablespoons (30 ml) orange juice
- 1 tablespoon (2 g) chopped fresh thyme
- 1 tablespoon (4 g) chopped fresh flat-leaf parsley
- ⅓ cup (80 ml) extra-virgin olive oil
- 1 teaspoon cocoa nibs

SALAD:
- ¼ cup toasted pine nuts
- 2 tablespoons (30 ml) olive oil
- 1 red onion, sliced thinly
- ½ teaspoon granulated sugar
- 4 cups (80 g) mixed salad greens
- 6 strawberries, hulled and sliced thinly

For the Asiago Cups: Preheat oven to 375°F (190°C, or gas mark 5). Spray a large cookie sheet with nonstick cooking spray or brush with vegetable oil. In a mixing bowl, combine the cheese with the cocoa nibs and pepper, tossing with your fingers to combine well. Drop four handfuls of cheese mixture onto the cookie sheet, pushing it out into 8-inch (20 cm) rounds. Place in the oven and bake for 12 minutes, or until melted and golden. Remove from oven and let stand for 1 minute. Working with a spatula or an offset spatula, carefully lift the cheese rounds from the pan and lay over the bottoms of glasses or ramekins, shaping into cups. Allow to cool completely on the molds.

For the Cocoa Balsamic Dressing: Combine all ingredients in a jar, cover tightly, and shake vigorously until combined.

Preheat oven to 350°F (180°C, or gas mark 4). Spread pine nuts on a sheet pan and bake for 4 minutes, until toasted and fragrant—be careful not to burn them. Remove from the oven and set aside to cool. Heat olive oil in a skillet over medium heat. Add the onion and cook, stirring occasionally, just until tender, about 5 minutes. Lower the heat to low, sprinkle onions with sugar, and allow to sweat for additional 5 minutes. Transfer to a plate to cool.

To prepare salad: Toss salad greens with dressing. Place an Asiago cup on a salad plate and fill, overflowing, with salad greens. Top greens with cooled onions, strawberries, and pine nuts.

Prep = 30 minutes **Cook** = 1 hour **Yield** = 4 servings

Twice-Baked Truffle Mashed Potatoes with White Chocolate

After you spend some time with this book, you may become obsessed with trying chocolate in everything, including the humble potato. Truffle-scented sea salt can be found in many gourmet food and kitchen stores. If it is not available, consider using truffle oil instead.

- 2 pounds (905 g) medium round Yukon gold potatoes
- 1/3 cup (80 g) sour cream
- 1/2 cup (120 ml) heavy cream
- 4 tablespoons (1/2 stick, or 55 g) unsalted butter, melted
- 1 teaspoon truffle-scented sea salt or truffle oil
- Black pepper
- 1 ounce (28 g) white chocolate, plus more for garnish
- 1/2 cup (58 g) shredded white cheddar cheese

Preheat oven to 400°F (200°C, or gas mark 6). Place potatoes on a baking sheet and bake for 45 minutes to 1 hour, until tender. Remove potatoes and let cool for 15 minutes, until able to handle. Cut potatoes in half, and scoop the flesh into a bowl, leaving about 1/4 inch (0.6 cm) thickness around sides of potato bowls.

In a small mixing bowl, whisk together the sour cream and heavy cream. Add the melted butter and combine. Add two-thirds of the sour cream mixture to the potatoes along with the truffle salt and black pepper. Mash potatoes to a creamy consistency, using a potato masher or fork. Grate in the chocolate and stir to combine. Spoon the potato mixture into the potato bowls, making heaping mounds, and top with a dollop of reserved sour cream mixture. Return the stuffed potatoes to the sheet pan and bake for 15 minutes. Remove from oven, turn oven to broil, sprinkle each potato bowl with shredded cheddar cheese, and broil tops until golden brown, just a couple of minutes. Remove and serve, dusted with more white chocolate.

Prep = 20 minute **Cook** = About 1 hour and 15 minutes
Yield = 4 servings

Sweet Potato–White Chocolate Soufflé

Remember: Never be intimidated by a soufflé. This is a great side dish for a special dinner. Make them in individual ramekins for great personal sides. The white chocolate is subtle, but it gives depth and a pleasant sweetness to the dish.

2	pounds (905 g) sweet potatoes (about 2 large potatoes)
1/2	cup (80 g) freshly grated Parmigiano-Reggiano cheese
3	tablespoons (42 g) unsalted butter
2	leeks, white parts only, diced
2	shallots, minced
1 1/2	cups (355 ml) milk
3	tablespoons (24 g) all-purpose flour
1/4	teaspoon freshly grated nutmeg
1/4	teaspoon ground allspice
1/4	teaspoon ground ginger
3	ounces (85 g) grated white chocolate
6	eggs, separated
1	cup (110 g) shredded Gruyère cheese
	Salt and freshly cracked black pepper

Preheat oven to 375°F (190°C, or gas mark 5). Pierce the potatoes several times with a fork and place on a baking sheet. Bake until tender, 30 to 40 minutes. Remove from the oven and let cool. Cut the sweet potatoes in half and scrape out the pulp into a mixing bowl. Using a potato masher, mash to form a smooth puree; you should have about 2½ cups (563 g) mashed sweet potato.

Evenly butter a 2-quart (2 L) soufflé dish or six 5-ounce (150 ml) ramekins and dust the bottom and sides with ¼ cup (40 g) of the Parmigiano-Reggiano cheese.

In a medium saucepan over medium heat, melt the butter. Add the leeks and shallots; sauté, stirring occasionally, until soft, about 10 minutes. Meanwhile, in a small saucepan over medium heat, warm the milk until small bubbles appear along the edges of the pan and steam begins to rise; remove from the heat. Add the flour to the leeks and cook, stirring constantly, for 3 minutes, just until tan (do not allow to brown). Whisk in the milk a little at a time and simmer, continuing to whisk, until thickened, 2 to 3 minutes. Remove from the heat and stir in the nutmeg, allspice, ginger, and grated white chocolate. Add the egg yolks one at a time, beating well after each addition. Add the mashed sweet potato and the Gruyère cheese, stirring until well incorporated. Season with salt and pepper to taste.

Using a stand mixer fitted with the whisk attachment, beat the egg whites on high speed just until stiff peaks form. Using a rubber spatula, fold the egg whites into the sweet potato mixture just to combine. Pour mixture into the buttered soufflé dish. Sprinkle evenly with remaining Parmigiano-Reggiano cheese. Place the soufflé on the middle rack of the oven and bake until puffed and golden, 45 to 50 minutes. If using ramekins, place them on a sheet pan and then bake. Serve warm.

Prep = About 45 minutes **Cook** = 45 to 50 minutes
Yield = 6 Servings

Chocolate Swirl Biscuits with Salt and Pepper Sugar

A cross between a biscuit and a cinnamon roll, this sweet dough recipe is a great way to start the morning. Bake on either a sheet pan or follow the alternative baking method below for individual pecan-topped biscuits.

1½ cups (180 g) all-purpose flour
½ cup (45 g) unsweetened cocoa powder
1 tablespoon (13 g) granulated sugar
1 tablespoon (14 g) baking powder
1 teaspoon baking soda
½ teaspoon salt
5 tablespoons (70 g) unsalted butter or margarine, cold, cut into small pieces
¾ cup plus 1 tablespoon (370 ml) whole milk

FILLING:
3 tablespoons (42 g) unsalted butter or margarine, softened
1½ tablespoons (19 g) granulated sugar

SALT AND PEPPER SUGAR TOPPING:
½ teaspoon granulated sugar
¼ teaspoon salt
¼ teaspoon ground black pepper
½ teaspoon ground cinnamon

Preheat oven to 400°F (200°C, or gas mark 6). Line a baking sheet with parchment paper or a Silpat. In a mixing bowl, whisk together the flour, cocoa powder, sugar, baking powder, baking soda, and salt. Add the pieces of cold butter and, using a pastry knife, cut the butter into the flour mixture until crumbly. Add the milk and, using a fork, stir mixture just until it comes together. Dust a dry, flat work surface with a mixture of flour and cocoa powder. Transfer the dough to the floured surface and flatten out into a rectangle. Roll the dough, dusting as needed, into a 10 x 16-inch (25 x 40 cm) rectangle. Spread the softened butter over the dough and then sprinkle with 1½ table-spoons (19 g) of sugar. Starting from the long side, begin to roll the dough into a semi-tight roll. Pinch the pieces together at the end and cut into twelve equal slices. Place the slices on the sheet pan. Combine all the ingredients for the topping in a small bowl and sprinkle over each slice. Bake on center rack of the oven for 15 to 18 minutes, until browned. Remove and serve warm.

Alternative baking method: Prepare recipe as directed above. Spray twelve standard-size muffin cups with nonstick cooking spray. Divide 2 teaspoons of sliced cold butter among the muffin cups, sprinkle ½ cup (55 g) of chopped pecans among the cups, and then sprinkle 3 tablespoons (38 g) of granulated sugar over the pecans in the cups. Place a biscuit into each muffin cup and press gently onto pecans. Sprinkle each with topping and bake on the middle rack for 15 to 18 minutes, until firm and toasted. Remove from the oven and invert onto a baking sheet; serve warm.

Prep = 15 minutes   **Cook** = 15 to 18 minutes   **Yield** = 12 biscuits

Black Bean and Chorizo Chili

Chocolate skeptics: Set aside some chili in a bowl before adding the chocolate. After adding the chocolate, do a taste test. Notice the difference?

- 5 tablespoons (75 ml) vegetable oil
- 1 pound (455 g) lean ground beef
- 1 large yellow onion, chopped
- 2 bell peppers, seeded and diced (1 green, 1 red)
- 4 cloves garlic, minced
- ½ pound (225 g) chorizo sausage, cut into quarters and sliced
- 1 (15.5 ounce, or 439 g) can black beans, rinsed and drained
- 1 (15.5 ounce, or 439 g) can red beans, rinsed and drained
- 1 (29 ounce, or 812 g) can crushed tomato
- 1 (15.5 ounce, or 439 g) can tomato sauce
- 3 cups (710 ml) beef stock
- 4 tablespoons (36 g) chili powder
- 2 tablespoons (18 g) ancho chili powder
- 2 tablespoons (8 g) dried oregano
- 2 tablespoons (14 g) ground cumin
- 1 teaspoon salt
- 1 teaspoon black pepper
- 1 ounce (28 g) bittersweet chocolate, chopped
- 1 cup (113 g) shredded sharp cheddar cheese, for garnish
- Crumbled corn chips or sliced green onions, for garnish

Heat 2 tablespoons (30 ml) vegetable oil in a large stockpot over medium-high heat. Add the ground beef and cook until browned through, about 5 minutes. Working with a spoon, break up the beef as it cooks. Transfer to a bowl, draining off any excess juices. Return stockpot to the heat, add the remaining 3 tablespoons (45 ml) of vegetable oil, and heat. Add the onion and peppers and cook, stirring occasionally, until tender, about 5 minutes. Add garlic and chorizo and cook until sausage is browned. Add the beans and crushed tomato. Cook for 5 minutes, stirring to combine. Add tomato sauce and stock. Bring to a boil, reduce heat, add the chile powders, oregano, cumin, salt, and black pepper. Simmer for 20 minutes, stirring occasionally. Add chocolate and cook for an additional 10 minutes. Serve hot with shredded cheese and crumbled tortilla chips.

Prep = 15 minutes **Cook** = 30 minutes **Yield** = 8 servings

Three-Bean Beef Chili

Bacon adds savory depth to this chili. If you like your chili spicy, toss in an extra jalapeno.

3   tablespoons (45 ml) olive oil
6   slices thick-cut smoked bacon, chopped
2   pounds (905 g) ground chuck
1   pound (455 g) ground buffalo or venison
1   large sweet yellow onion, chopped
1   large red onion, chopped
2   green bell peppers, seeded and chopped
6   cloves garlic, minced
1   jalapeño, seeded and minced
⅓   cup (30 g) chili powder
2   tablespoons (14 g) ground cumin
1   tablespoon (4 g) dried oregano
1   tablespoon (7 g) smoked paprika
1   cup (235 ml) dry red wine
6   cups (1.4 L) beef stock
1   can (14.5 ounce, or 411 g) crushed tomatoes
1   can (15.5 ounce, or 439 g) red kidney beans, rinsed and drained
1   can (15.5 ounce, or 439 g) cannelini beans, rinsed and drained
1   can (15.5 ounce, or 439 g) pinto beans, rinsed and drained
3   tablespoons (36 g) masa harina or fine yellow cornmeal
3   ounces (85 g) dark chocolate, grated
    Shredded cheddar cheese, for garnish
    Crumbled corn tortilla chips, for garnish

In a large stockpot heat the oil over medium-high heat. Add the bacon, cooking until just turning crisp; add the ground chuck and buffalo. Cook the beef until browned through, crumbling with the spoon as it cooks. Add the onion and peppers and cook until just tender, about 4 minutes. Add the garlic and jalapeno, cooking for 2 minutes. Add the chili powder, cumin, oregano, and paprika, cooking for 2 minutes. Add the red wine, scraping up the bits on the bottom of the pan as it cooks. Add the stock, tomatoes, and beans, stirring to combine. Bring to a boil, add masa harina, reduce heat and simmer for 30 minutes. Add grated chocolate, stirring to incorporate. Serve hot topped with shredded cheddar cheese and crumbled corn tortilla chips.

Prep = 30 minutes   **Cook** = 30 minutes   **Yield** = 6 to 8 Servings

Black Bean Soft Tacos with Simple Mole

These tacos use the mole recipe on page 176. Hard corn shells can be used in the recipe if you prefer.

1   (15.5 ounce, or 439 g) can black beans, drained
3   strips bacon, cooked and chopped
4   tablespoons (60 ml) quick mole (page 176)
1   teaspoon ground cumin
1   teaspoon dried oregano
1/2 teaspoon salt
1/4 teaspoon black pepper

1   cup (70 g) coleslaw mix
1   tablespoon (15 ml) fresh lime juice
2   green onions, sliced thinly
1/3 cup (20 g) chopped fresh cilantro
8   flour tortillas
1/2 cup (75 g) crumbled feta cheese

In a bowl, toss the black beans with cooked bacon, mole, cumin, salt, and black pepper. In another bowl, toss the coleslaw mix with the lime juice, green onions, and cilantro. Lay out flour tortillas on a clean, dry work surface. Spoon the coleslaw mix onto each of them and top evenly with black bean mixture and then crumbled feta cheese. Roll and serve. If you like, add chicken from Braised Chicken Mole (page 176). Simply shred the chicken and place on top of beans.

Prep = 20 minutes   **Yield** = 4 servings

Chicken and Poblano Enchiladas with White Chocolate

The hint of white chocolate gives the sauce in these enchiladas a subtle sweetness and velvety creaminess. Classic mole uses dark chocolate, so I tried a verde with white chocolate. Store-bought tomatillo (or any green salsa) makes a flavorful sauce without hours of preparation. These enchiladas can be made in 30 minutes for a weeknight meal or a day ahead of time for weekend entertaining.

8	flour tortillas
2	(6-ounce, 170 g) chicken breasts, cooked and sliced very thinly
1	teaspoon ground cumin
1/4	teaspoon salt
1/4	teaspoon fresh ground black pepper
1	cup (225 g) green tomatillo salsa
1	cup (230 g) sour cream
1/4	cup (60 ml) chicken stock
1	tablespoon (7 g) ground cumin
1	ounce (28 g) white chocolate, melted
2	tablespoons (8 g) chopped fresh cilantro
2	scallions, sliced thinly
1	tablespoon (15 ml) vegetable or olive oil
1	large yellow onion, chopped
1	poblano pepper, seeded and chopped
2	cups (240 g) shredded Monterey Jack cheese
2	cups (225 g) shredded cheddar cheese
1/2	cup (90 g) black beans
	Black bean tortilla chips, crumbled

Preheat oven to 375°F (190°C, or gas mark 5). Lightly grease an 11 × 7-inch (27.5 × 17.5 cm) glass baking dish and set aside. Toss the chicken in a bowl with the cumin, salt, and pepper; set aside. In a large saucepan over medium-high heat, combine the salsa, sour cream, chicken stock, cumin, and white chocolate, stirring until warmed and smooth. Stir in the cilantro and scallion; remove from heat. In a small sauté pan, heat the oil over medium-high heat and sauté the onion and pepper until tender, about 4 minutes. Remove from the heat and set aside to cool. Combine the two cheeses in a bowl, transfer 1 cup (120 g) of cheese to another bowl and set aside for the top of the enchiladas. Mix the black beans with the cooled onions and peppers. Place ½ cup (115 g) of the sour cream sauce in the prepared pan, smoothing out to cover the bottom of the pan. Begin to roll the enchiladas. Get all of the ingredients in front of you—working with four flour tortillas at a time, lay them out. Line each down the middle with shredded chicken, top with the onion mixture and then with a sprinkle of cheese. Roll up the tortillas and place tightly together in the prepared dish. Repeat with the remaining ingredients, placing tightly in the dish. Cover the enchiladas with remaining sauce, spreading out to cove the edges. Sprinkle evenly with reserved 1 cup of cheese and then with the crumbled tortilla chips. Place in the oven and bake for 20 minutes, until cheese is thoroughly melted and browned a bit on top. Remove, let rest for 10 minutes, and serve immediately. This can be made up to 1 day ahead of time without cooking. Wrap and refrigerate. Remove from the refrigerator 30 minutes prior to cooking.

Prep = 30 minutes   **Cook** = 20 minutes   **Yield** =4 servings

Braised Chicken Mole

Mole has as many variations as there are towns in Mexico. The classic version has dried peppers, nuts, herbs and spices, and its trademark: chocolate.

5 tablespoons (75 ml) olive oil
8 chicken pieces
1 sweet yellow onion, diced
1 red bell pepper, seeded and diced
3 cloves fresh garlic, minced
1 tablespoon (8 g) sesame seeds
2 tablespoons (18 g) chili powder
1 tablespoon (9 g) ancho chili powder
2 teaspoons ground cumin
1 teaspoon ground cinnamon
1 tablespoon (2 g) dried marjoram
¼ cup (30 g) finely chopped almonds
¼ cup (40 g) finely chopped raisins
1 (15.5-ounce, 439 g) can diced roasted tomatoes
2 chipotle peppers in adobo sauce, chopped
2 tablespoons (32 g) creamy peanut butter
2 cups (475 ml) chicken broth
3 ounces (85 g) bittersweet chocolate, grated

Preheat oven to 375°F (190°C, or gas mark 5). Heat 3 tablespoons of the olive oil in a large Dutch oven (with a lid). Sear the chicken in the hot oil, browning on all sides. Place in a Dutch oven and set aside.

For the Mole: In a large skillet, heat the remaining olive oil over medium-high heat. Add the onion and pepper and sauté until tender, about 3 minutes. Add the garlic and sesame seeds, cooking for 1 minute. Add the chili powders, cumin, cinnamon, marjoram, almonds, and raisins; cook for 3 minutes, until aromatic. Add the tomatoes, chipotle peppers, and peanut butter. Bring to a slow boil and add the chicken broth; return to boil, then reduce to a simmer. Add the chocolate, stir to combine, simmer for 20 minutes. Strain mixture into a blender and puree until smooth—blend in batches if necessary. Pour the mixture over chicken, cover, and place in oven to roast for 1 hour, until the meat is pulling away from the bone. Serve over rice.

Prep = 30 minutes   **Cook** = 1 hour   **Yield** = 8 servings

Jerked Chicken with Chocolate Island Sauce

Cooking this chicken on the grill gives it a smoky flavor and crisp texture. Spicy and succulent, the chicken is fantastic on its own, but the mango salsa and chocolate sauce make this an island treat for any occasion.

4	(6-ounce, 170 g) pieces of chicken breast, pounded a bit to flatten
	Salt
	Freshly ground black pepper
1/4	cup (32 g) jerk seasoning
1	mango, peeled and diced
3	scallions, sliced thinly on the diagonal
1	jalapeño, seeds and veins removed and minced
1/2	cup (80 g) chopped red onion
1/2	cup (60 g) chopped red pepper
2	tablespoons (28 ml) orange juice
1/2	cup (120 ml) chicken stock
1/2	cup (120 ml) mango nectar
1	tablespoon (15 ml) balsamic vinegar
1/2	teaspoon ground cumin
1/2	teaspoon chili powder
2	ounces (55 g) dark chocolate

Place the chicken on a platter and season with salt and pepper, then season generously with jerk seasoning; set aside for 30 minutes. Preheat grill to high heat. In a bowl, mix together the mango, scallions, jalapeño, red onion, red pepper, and orange juice. Season with salt and black pepper. Place the chicken on the grill, cooking for 8 minutes per side, until a meat thermometer inserted in the center of one breast registers at least 165°F (74°C). Transfer to a platter. In a saucepan over medium-high heat, mix together the chicken stock, mango nectar, balsamic vinegar, cumin, and chili powder; bring to a boil, reduce the heat to simmer. Let simmer for 20 minutes, reducing the liquid. Remove from heat, stir in the chocolate until melted and smooth, season with salt and black pepper, and pour over grilled chicken. Top chicken with mango salsa and serve.

Prep = 30 minutes **Cook** = 16 minutes **Yield** = 4 servings

Cocoa Pork with Apple Slaw

Searing the pork locks in the moisture while creating a delicious crust, due in part to the sugar and cocoa in the rub. The flavors have great depth with a hint of spice from the chili powder. If you like, cook a whole loin or tenderloin with this rub, then serve the sliced pork and slaw in hearty sandwiches.

DRY RUB:

- 1/2 teaspoon ancho chili powder
- 1/4 teaspoon salt
- 1 tablespoon (15 g) brown sugar
- 1/2 teaspoon ground black pepper
- 1/4 teaspoon ground cinnamon
- 1 1/2 teaspoons dried rosemary, crumbled
- 2 teaspoons cocoa nibs (optional)
- 1 1/2 teaspoons unsweetened cocoa powder

- 4 pork loin steaks or bone-in pork chops

APPLE SLAW:

- 3 Braeburn apples, peeled and grated (or other tart, crisp apples)
  Juice of 1/2 lemon
- 4 cups (280 g) thinly sliced white cabbage
- 4 scallions, green and white parts, cut into 2-inch (5.1 cm) pieces and then sliced thin
- 1/2 cup (115 g) sour cream
- 1/4 cup (60 g) plain yogurt
- 1 tablespoon (15 ml) olive oil
- 2 tablespoons (30 g) firmly packed light brown sugar
- 1 1/2 tablespoons (30 g) honey
- 2 tablespoons (28 ml) cider vinegar
- 1/4 teaspoon salt
- 1/2 teaspoon ground black pepper
- 2 tablespoons (8 g) chopped flat-leaf parsley
- 1/2 cup (60 g) chopped walnuts, toasted

Preheat a grill to high heat. Combine all ingredients for dry rub. Rub both sides of all pieces of pork with the dry rub and set aside.

For the Apple Slaw: Grate the apples into a bowl and toss with the lemon juice. In a large bowl, combine the cabbage, apples, and scallions; toss to mix. In a small bowl whisk together the sour cream, yogurt, olive oil, brown sugar, honey, cider vinegar, salt, pepper, parsley, and walnuts. Pour over apple mixture, tossing to coat evenly; cover with plastic wrap and refrigerate until ready to serve.

Place the pork on the grill, cooking for about 5 minutes per side, rotating halfway through to create crisscrossing grill marks. Remove from the grill, let rest for 5 minutes; serve atop a bed of slaw.

Prep = 30 minutes **Cook** = About 10 minutes **Yield** = 4 servings

Slow-Roasted Cocoa Pepper Pork Tenderloin

A quick and simple dinner preparation, this pork dish develops a crisp crust with a juicy, tender center. For advance prep, dry rub the tenderloin, cover, and refrigerate until the next day's dinner. Remove it from the refrigerator and let sit for 30 minutes prior to cooking.

COCOA PEPPER RUB:

- 1   tablespoon (6 g) unsweetened cocoa powder
- 1¹⁄₂ teaspoons freshly ground black pepper
- 1   teaspoon paprika
- 1   tablespoon (13 g) granulated sugar
- ¹⁄₂ teaspoon sea salt

1 to 2   pounds (455 to 905 g) pork tenderloin, cleaned and dried

Combine all the ingredients for the rub in a small bowl. Rub the pork tenderloin generously with the rub, cover, and refrigerate for at least 1 hour. Remove from refrigerator 15 minutes before cooking. Preheat a grill to high heat or, alternatively, preheat oven to 375°F (190°C, or gas mark 5). If using the grill, once the grill is hot, place the tenderloin on the grill and sear all sides of the tenderloin for about 5 minutes per side; reduce the heat to low and cook the tenderloin until it reaches an internal temperature of 130°F (54°C) for rare or 145°F (63°C) for well done. Remove the tenderloin and let rest for 5 minutes before slicing to serve. If using the oven, heat 2 tablespoons (30 ml) of vegetable oil in a large skillet over high heat. Sear the tenderloin on all sides in the pan, about 3 minutes per side. Once all sides are seared, place pan in the oven on middle rack; cook for 20 minutes, until internal temperature is the same as for the grill. Remove from the oven and let rest for 5 minutes before slicing to serve.

Prep = 1 hour **Cook** = 30 minutes **Yield** = 4 servings

Chocolate-Chipotle Ribs

Once summer rolls around, I am known in my circles for my barbecued ribs. These use chocolate only in the grilling sauce, but the results are tremendous. They may make your ribs just as popular among your friends.

2   pounds (905 g, or 2 racks) pork baby back ribs
    Cocoa Pepper Rub (page 180)
2   cups (475 ml) Chocolate Touched Barbecue Sauce (page 158)
2   chipotle peppers, chopped
2   ounces (55 g) bittersweet chocolate, melted

Soak for at least 1 hour, as many untreated cedar shingles as will cover the entire cooking surface of your grill. Rinse the ribs and pat dry; rub thoroughly with the dry rub, getting into all of the surfaces. Cover and refrigerate for at least 1 hour. Remove from the refrigerator 30 minutes prior to grilling. Preheat grill to high heat for 20 minutes. Reduce grill heat to low, place soaked cedar shingles on grill and place ribs on top of shingles. Close grill and leave alone for 1 hour. Combine the barbecue sauce with chipotle peppers and melted chocolate. After 1 hour of cooking, slather sauce mixture over ribs, coating both sides. Close lid and cook an additional 2 hours. Slather the sauce on ribs every 30 minutes.

A note of caution: When you open the grill cover, that is when fire can kick up on the shingles. It's a good idea to have a spray bottle of water to moisten the shingles during cooking. If you have extra shingles, you can always slide additional soaked shingles under the burning ones. The ribs are done when the meat pulls away from the bone. Everyone's grill is different, so ribs may be done in the 3 hours or may take longer. Remove from grill, cut into pieces, and serve.

Prep = 20 minutes   **Cook** = 3 or more hours   **Yield** = 4 servings

Hamburgers with Chopped Bacon and Cocoa Nibs

Grilling is my favorite way to cook. I am the only one in the neighborhood who doesn't wrap up and shut down the grill for the winter. For these burgers, I added plenty of flavor with Worcestershire sauce, chopped scallions, and bacon, but the surprise addition is the cocoa nibs.

4	strips bacon, chopped
2	tablespoons (30 ml) vegetable oil
1	large red onion, sliced thinly
1	pound (455 g) ground sirloin
4	scallions, minced
½	cup (50 g) cocoa nibs
1	teaspoon salt
1	teaspoon ground black pepper
1	teaspoon Worcestershire sauce
2	tablespoons (30 ml) vegetable oil
4	slices cheddar cheese
4	hamburger buns, split

Preheat grill to high heat. In a large skillet, cook the bacon over medium heat until browned, transfer to paper towel to drain and cool; reserve the bacon grease. In the same skillet, heat the bacon grease with the vegetable oil. Add the onion and cook for 1 minute, reduce heat to low, and let the onion sweat for 5 minutes, just until tender; transfer to a plate and set aside. In a mixing bowl, combine the ground sirloin with the crumbled bacon, scallions, cocoa nibs, salt, black pepper, and Worcestershire sauce. Working with your hands, mash and work the mixture until all ingredients are combined. Form into patties. Spray each patty with nonstick cooking spray and grill 5 minutes on each side for medium-rare and longer for well done. When there is 3 minutes left of cooking time, top each burger with cheese and melt. Build each burger with the buns and lettuce, tomato, or any accompaniment you like.

Prep = 20 minutes   **Cook** = 15 minutes   **Yield** = 4 servings

Pepper Tenderloin Steaks with Cherry-Chocolate Sauce

Ever wonder how restaurants get Steak au Poivre so perfect, with a coating of what seems to be peppercorn bread crumbs? The trick is to use cracked peppercorns, not ground. Cracked peppercorns are coarser and more flavorful than pepper ground in a mill. The best way to do it, and this takes patience, is to use a mini-food processor and pulse fresh peppercorns until they're cracked into thick pieces. For best results, pick out the uncracked peppercorns and repeat the process. I store a jar of peppercorns and use for all of my steak grilling.

⅓ cup (30 g) cracked peppercorns
Sea salt to taste
4 beef tenderloin steaks (10 to 12 ounces, or 280 to 340 g each)
3 tablespoons (45 ml) canola oil
2 cups (475 ml) Chocolate Cherry Port Sauce (page 159)

Preheat oven to 500°F (250°C, or gas mark 10). Press pepper and generous amount of salt into both sides of all four steaks and set aside. Heat the canola oil in a large skillet over high heat. Place the steaks in the skillet without crowding them, and cook uncovered for about 3 minutes per side, browning but not charring. Transfer to a baking sheet and place in the oven to continue cooking for 8 minutes for medium-rare, longer for well-done. While the steaks are cooking, pour the port sauce into the skillet where you cooked the steaks, and heat through, scraping the bottom of the pan. Serve the steaks topped with Chocolate Cherry Port Sauce.

Prep = 20 minutes **Cook** = 15 minutes **Yield** = 4 servings

Cocoa and Coffee-Roasted Rib Eye with Morels

Rib eye steaks, with all of their marbling, are the most flavorful steaks. If you can afford the luxury of dry-aged rib eye, do so—it is worth the experience, especially for this rich sauce of cocoa and balsamic vinegar. The morels are a fantastic mushroom, with an earthy flavor and a robust texture. If you can't find morels, substitute with shitake or cremini, or even slices of portabello.

3	tablespoons (45 ml) olive oil
4	cloves garlic, minced
3	shallots, chopped
1/2	cup (120 ml) balsamic vinegar
2	teaspoons honey
1	tablespoon (6 g) unsweetened cocoa powder
1	teaspoon instant espresso powder dissolved in 2 tablespoons (28 ml) hot water
1/4	teaspoon sea salt
1/2	teaspoon fresh ground black pepper
24	fresh morel mushrooms, brushed clean
1	teaspoon freshly ground pepper
3/4	teaspoon salt
2	tablespoons (28 g) unsalted butter, cut into bits
2	tablespoons (4 g) coarsely chopped fresh rosemary
4	boneless rib-eye steaks, each about 5 ounces (140 g) and 1/2 inch (1.3 cm) thick

In a small saucepan, heat the olive oil over medium heat. Add the garlic and shallots and sauté for 2 minutes. Add the balsamic vinegar, honey, cocoa powder, and espresso powder mixed with water; stir until smooth. Let reduce for 5 minutes, season with salt and black pepper; set aside to cool. Once cooled, pour three quarters of the sauce (reserving the rest for finishing sauce) over steaks in a shallow dish to marinate; cover and refrigerate for at least 30 minutes and up to 1 hour. Remove from the refrigerator 15 minutes prior to grilling.

Heat a grill to high heat. Place a cast-iron skillet on the grill to preheat. Toss the morel mushrooms with ground pepper and salt. Place the mushrooms in the skillet with the butter and 2 tablespoons (4 g) chopped rosemary. Cook until the mushrooms are tender and its juices are running. Remove from the grill or set aside on a cool side of the grill.

While the mushrooms are cooking, place the steaks on the hot portion of the grill, searing on each side for 2 minutes. Then move to a cooler side of the grill and continue to cook on each side for 2 to 3 additional minutes, turning to create grill marks. Remove from the grill and let rest for 5 minutes. Serve topped with mushrooms and a drizzle of the reserved sauce.

Prep = 30 minutes   **Cook** = 15 minutes   **Yield** = 4 servings

Espresso-Cocoa Nib Flank Steak with Olive Chimichurri

The surprise in this dish is the pairing of olives and chocolate.

ESPRESSO-COCOA NIB DRY RUB:

1	teaspoon instant espresso powder
1	tablespoon (6 g) cocoa nibs, ground in a spice grinder
½	teaspoon chili powder
1	teaspoon Spanish paprika
½	teaspoon sea salt
1	teaspoon coarse ground black pepper

Pinch of ground nutmeg

1 to 2	pounds (455 to 905 g) flank steak

CHIMICHURRI:

3	tablespoons (45 ml) extra-virgin olive oil
4	garlic cloves, sliced thinly
¼	teaspoon dried crushed red pepper
1	bay leaf, broken
⅓	cup (53 g) finely chopped red onion
¼	cup (15 g) finely chopped fresh flat-leaf parsley
2	scallions (green tops only), finely minced
2	tablespoons (20 g) finely chopped pitted kalamata olives
1	teaspoon orange zest
2	tablespoons (30 ml) white balsamic vinegar
1	tablespoon (15 ml) water (or more if needed to thin)

In a small bowl combine all ingredients for the rub. Rub the flank steak on all sides with the dry rub and set aside for at least 1 hour.

For the Chimichurri: In a sauté pan, heat olive oil over medium heat; sauté garlic with the red pepper and bay leaf for 1 minute. Add the onion and sauté until translucent. Remove from the heat and remove the bay leaf. Stir in the parsley, scallions, olives, zest, vinegar, and water (add more water if needed). Set aside until ready to serve. Preheat a grill to high heat. Brush the flank steak on both sides with olive oil. Grill for 7 minutes per side for medium-rare. Remove from grill and let rest for 5 minutes, slice thinly, and top with Chimichurri.

Prep = 10 minutes **Cook** = 14 minutes **Yield** = 6 servings

Yogurt Marinated Lamb Kabobs with Indian Cocoa Rub

The yogurt marinade softens the gamey flavor of the lamb while the chocolate and spices give it a burst of flavor. The cocoa nibs, if you have them, add a great texture to the lamb after it is grilled.

2 cups (490 g) plain yogurt
1½ cups (355 ml) water
¼ cup (15 g) chopped fresh mint
2 pounds (905 g) trimmed boneless leg of lamb, cut into 1½-inch (3.8 cm) cubes
Salt and black pepper
1½ teaspoons ancho chile powder
1 teaspoon turmeric
1 tablespoon (6 g) unsweetened cocoa powder
1 large garlic clove, minced
1 tablespoon (6 g) cocoa nibs (optional)
½ teaspoon cayenne
1 ounce (28 g) square of Ancho Grating Chocolate (page 152) or premium dark chocolate, for garnish
Zest of 1 lemon
2 tablespoons (30 ml) fresh lemon juice

In a large bowl, mix together 1 cup (245 g) of the yogurt, water, and mint. Add the lamb cubes, tossing to coat. Cover and refrigerate for at least 6 hours and up to overnight.

Preheat the grill or broiler to high. Remove the lamb cubes from marinade and pat dry; season with salt and a generous amount of pepper. In a bowl, combine the remaining 1 cup (245 g) of yogurt with the chile powder, turmeric, cocoa powder, garlic, cocoa nibs, and cayenne. Add the lamb and toss to coat evenly; set aside for 15 minutes. Thread lamb cubes evenly on six metal skewers. Season with salt and generously with freshly ground black pepper. Grill the skewers over high heat, turning until charred all over, 7 to 8 minutes total for medium-rare. Transfer to a platter and sprinkle with grated chocolate and lemon zest and juice. Serve hot with rice.

Prep = 20 minutes **Marinate** = 6 hours **Cook** = 7 minutes
Yield = 6 servings

Ancho Seared Scallops with Chocolate Balsamic Sauce

With just a little seasoning and a sauce of chocolate and balsamic, it might seem that you slaved for hours to achieve this restaurant-quality gourmet dish. Refrigerate leftover sauce in an airtight container for up to five days.

16	sea scallops cleaned
1	tablespoon (9 g) ancho chile powder
1/2	teaspoon ground cumin
1/2	teaspoon sea salt
1/2	teaspoon fresh ground black pepper
8	slices lean bacon
4	tablespoons (60 ml) olive oil
2	large sweet Vidalia onions, cut in half and then sliced very thinly
4	ounces (115 g) premium dark chocolate
1/4	cup (60 ml) good-quality balsamic vinegar
2	teaspoons apple cider vinegar
1/2	cup (120 ml) pineapple juice

Pat the sea scallops dry and set aside. In a small bowl combine the ancho chile powder, cumin, salt, and pepper. Dust the scallops with the spice mixture on both sides and set aside. In a large skillet, fry the bacon until crisp, and transfer to a paper towel to drain, leaving the bacon grease in the pan. Return the pan to medium-high heat and add 1 tablespoon (15 ml) of the olive oil. Add the onions and sauté for 1 minute. Reduce heat to low and sweat the onions for 5 minutes, or until tender. Remove and set aside. Add 3 tablespoons (45 ml) olive oil to skillet over high heat. Place the scallops in the hot oil, searing for 2 minutes per side. Transfer to a paper towel to drain. Place the chocolate in a heatproof bowl. In a saucepan over medium heat, combine the balsamic vinegar, apple cider vinegar, and pineapple juice; heat until just beginning to bubble. Pour mixture over chocolate, let stand for 1 minute, then whisk until melted and smooth. Cut the bacon into sixteen strips, place on plate, and top with a scallop, then with onions, and then drizzle Chocolate Balsamic Sauce. Serve hot.

Prep = 20 minutes **Cook** = 15 minutes **Yield** =4 servings

Salt-Roasted Shrimp with White Chocolate Balsamic Dipping Sauce

Salt-roasting fish and shellfish locks in the sweetness and moisture of the food. These shrimp are a perfect appetizer or cocktail dish with a creamy, sweet, and tangy dipping sauce of white chocolate and white balsamic vinegar.

4½ cups (1.3 kg) kosher salt
2 pounds (905 g) unshelled large shrimp

WHITE CHOCOLATE BALSAMIC DIPPING SAUCE:
4 ounces (115 g) white chocolate, chopped
¼ cup (60 ml) white balsamic vinegar
½ cup (120 ml) mango nectar
Generous amount of sea salt and freshly ground black pepper

Preheat oven to 500°F (250°C, or gas mark 10). Pour the salt into a large cast-iron skillet and heat in the oven for 20 minutes, until very hot. Turn the oven off but keep the door closed. Place the shrimp in a single layer in a large, deep baking dish (two if necessary). Pour the hot salt over the shrimp, covering them entirely. Place in the oven and cook for 5 minutes, until just cooked through. Rinse the shrimp under hot water and pat dry. Serve immediately with the White Chocolate Balsamic Dipping Sauce.

For the White Chocolate Balsamic Dipping Sauce: Place the white chocolate in a heatproof bowl. Heat the balsamic vinegar and mango nectar in a saucepan until steaming and just beginning to bubble. Pour over the white chocolate in a bowl, let sit for 2 minutes, then whisk until melted and smooth. Season with salt and black pepper.

Prep = 20 minutes **Cook** = 25 minutes **Yield** = 6 servings

Shrimp with Scallion and Chocolate-Balsamic Sauce

The rich taste of balsamic vinegar pairs perfectly with dark chocolate. I've combined them in a decadent sauce that could be served with beef or poultry in addition to shrimp. If you're preparing food for guests, just double the recipe.

3	ounces (85 g) premium dark chocolate
2	tablespoons (28 g) unsalted butter, softened
5	tablespoons (75 ml) olive oil
2	tablespoons (30 ml) premium balsamic vinegar
1½	pounds (680 g) large, 13/15-size shrimp, peeled and deveined
	Sea salt and fresh ground black pepper
3	shallots, chopped finely
2	cloves fresh garlic, minced
6	scallions, sliced thinly on the diagonal (whites and greens)

For the sauce: In the top of a double boiler, melt the chocolate with the butter and 2 tablespoons (30 ml) of the olive oil. Once melted, remove from heat and gradually, in a steady stream, whisk in the balsamic vinegar until incorporated; set aside and keep warm.

Toss the shrimp in a bowl with generous amounts of sea salt and freshly ground black pepper, coating evenly. Heat the remaining 3 tablespoons (45 ml) of olive oil in a large skillet over medium-high heat. Add the shallot and garlic, sautéing just until tender. Add the shrimp, sautéing just until they turn pink. Add the scallion, cooking for 1 minute. Remove the pan from the heat and add the chocolate-balsamic sauce, stirring to coat the shrimp. Remove from the heat and serve with wild rice.

Prep = 15 minutes **Cook** = 15 minutes **Yield** = 4 servings

Ravioli with Crab and White Chocolate Sage Butter

Using prepared, store-bought ravioli for this dish makes it a quick and simple yet tasty weeknight dinner. Any pasta will work, but the ravioli make it a heartier dish. Use a premium quality crab for the best flavor. Fresh sage leaves are a must for this dish. Dried sage just won't do.

Store-bought ravioli (sweet potato, cheese, spinach)

6 tablespoons (83 g) unsalted butter

3 shallots, minced

12 whole, fresh sage leaves

9 ounces (255 g) lump crabmeat, picked over for shells

2 tablespoons (14 g) unseasoned bread crumbs

4 tablespoons (56 ml) olive oil

1 tablespoon (4 g) minced fresh flat-leaf parsley

Sea salt

Pinch ground white pepper

2 ounces (55 g) white chocolate, divided

Parmigiano-Reggiano cheese, for garnish

Bring a large saucepan of water to a boil. Cook ravioli according to package instructions. Drain and keep warm. In a large skillet melt the butter over medium heat. Add the shallots and sage leaves, cooking until the shallots are just tender. Add the crab and bread crumbs, cooking until the bread crumbs become toasted. Add olive oil and parsley and heat through. Season with sea salt and pepper, and grate 1 ounce (28 g) of the white chocolate, using a microplane grater, into the pan, stirring to combine. Spoon crab mixture over ravioli, grating Parmigiano-Reggiano and additional white chocolate on top. Serve immediately.

Prep = 15 minutes **Cook** = 10 minutes **Yield** = 4 servings

6

Beverages and Frozen Desserts

Mocha Latte Smoothie

Indulge yourself in rich mocha with a fresh twist—a mocha latte smoothie. Combining the tastes of coffee and chocolate elevate this smoothie from the everyday to the extra special. I enjoy this year-round, as a summer treat or rich winter sweet.

$\frac{1}{2}$ cup (120 ml) fat-free chocolate milk
1 cup (235 ml) chilled coffee
$\frac{1}{2}$ cup (125 g) nonfat vanilla yogurt
1 scoop chocolate ice cream
8 ice cubes
Chocolate Syrup (page 230)

Combine first five ingredients in a blender and blend on high-speed until smooth. Drizzle chocolate syrup inside a tall, clear glass; pour smoothie, and serve.

Prep = 10 minutes   **Yield** = 1 (10-ounce [280 ml]) smoothie

Chocolate Morning Smoothie

Using protein powder (such as whey protein) makes a smoothie a nutritious meal alternative. Today you can find protein powders in just about every supermarket; choose one that is right for your dietary situation and goals. Whey protein in chocolate or vanilla flavors are versatile choices.

3	scoops chocolate-flavored protein powder
$\frac{1}{2}$	cup (120 ml) skim milk
$\frac{1}{2}$	cup (120 ml) fat-free chocolate milk
$\frac{1}{2}$	cup (125 g) nonfat vanilla yogurt
2	tablespoons (32 g) creamy peanut butter
1	ripe banana, sliced
6	ice cubes

Combine all ingredients in a blender and blend until smooth; scrape down the sides if necessary. Serve immediately.

Variation: For spicier fare first thing in the morning, add $\frac{1}{2}$ teaspoon of ground nutmeg, cinnamon, or ginger. Alternatively, substitute the ripe banana for $\frac{1}{2}$ cup (73 g) of strawberries, blueberries, or any other fruit in season.

Prep = 10 minutes   **Yield** = 1 (10-ounce [280 ml]) smoothie

Berry Blast Smoothie

The frozen-foods department of your grocery store is a great place to find perfect fruits and berries year-round. Gourmet grocers will have an even broader, more exotic selection. Here I have combined strawberries, blueberries, and raspberries for a berry blast. Vary the berry combination to your preferences.

2	scoops vanilla whey protein powder
1/2	cup(125 g) nonfat vanilla yogurt
1	cup (235 ml) skim milk
1/2	cup (40 g) rolled oats (not cooked)
4	large strawberries
1/4	cup (39 g) frozen blueberries
1/4	cup (31 g) frozen raspberries
6	ice cubes

Combine all ingredients in a blender and blend until smooth. Drink immediately or refrigerate for up to one day.

Prep = 10 minutes   **Yield** = 1 (10-ounce [285 ml]) smoothie

Chocolate Liqueur

Vodka infused with chocolate and sugar becomes a rich, thick liqueur. Enjoyed as a chilled shot, a dash in hot cocoa, or to flavor ganache, homemade chocolate liqueur will be a welcome addition to your drink repertoire. All the ingredients are most likely already in your pantry.

- ½ cup (45 g) unsweetened cocoa powder
- 2 cups (475 ml) boiling water
- 2 cups (400 g) granulated sugar
- 2 cups (475 ml) water
- 2 cups (475 ml) vodka

In a medium bowl, stir together the cocoa powder and boiling water until dissolved; set aside. In a small saucepan, combine the sugar and water and bring to a simmer, stirring until the sugar has dissolved. Add the sugar syrup to the cocoa mixture, stirring to combine. Add the vodka and stir. Strain the mixture through a fine-mesh sieve, into a container with a tight lid. Refrigerate the mixture overnight, and store for several weeks.

To serve, stir the liqueur well, then strain it again through a fine-mesh sieve. Serve as chilled shots topped with cream and cinnamon or use in cocktails.

Prep = 10 minutes   **Chill** = At least 8 hours   **Yield** = 6 cups

Wedding Cake Martini

There is a Southern wedding tradition called the Groom's Cake, which calls for a chocolate version of the wedding cake to be served alongside the traditional wedding cake. It was always my favorite at weddings. Although it's not so typical anymore, I decided to bring back the Groom's Cake in this fanciful cocktail.

- **6** tablespoons (26 g) sweetened flaked coconut
- **2** lime wedges
  Splash of cranberry juice
- **3** ounces (90 ml) pineapple juice
- **3** ounces (90 ml) vanilla vodka
- **2** ounces (60 ml) white crème de cacao
- **2** maraschino cherries, for garnish

Preheat oven to 350°F (180°C, or gas mark 4); spread sweetened coconut flakes in an even layer across a sheet pan. Place in oven and bake until golden brown, 5 to 7 minutes, being careful not to burn it. Remove from the oven and let cool and dry out for about 30 minutes. Place coconut in a food processor and grind to a coarse consistency. Place on a flat plate, coat the rim of each glass with lime juice by running the lime wedge around the rim of the glass, and plunge the rim of the glass into the toasted coconut, coating evenly; set aside.

Fill a large cocktail shaker with ice cubes. Pour all liquid ingredients into shaker and shake vigorously. Strain into the cocktail glasses and garnish each with a cherry.

Prep = 10 minutes   **Yield** = 2 cocktails

Chocolate Cake Martini

I was once a judge for a cocktail competition. The variety of concoctions was staggering, but with the multitude of liqueurs on the shelves, it is no wonder there are so many drink options. This once came to mind after having a "Wedding Cake" cocktail—why not chocolate cake? Enjoy!

3 ounces (90 ml) vanilla vodka
2 ounces (60 ml) crème de cacao
½ ounce (14 ml) Frangelico hazelnut liqueur
1 ounce (28 ml) chocolate liqueur
1 tablespoon (6 g) sweetened cocoa powder
2 lemon twists

Fill two cocktail glasses with ice water and set aside to chill.

Fill a large cocktail shaker with ice, and add vanilla vodka, creme de cacao, Frangelico hazelnut liqueur, and chocolate liqueur. Shake vigorously. Empty glasses of ice water, and dip the edges into a flat dish filled with sweetened cocoa powder. Strain the contents of the cocktail shaker into the two cocktail glasses, and add a twist of lemon to each before serving.

Prep = 5 minutes **Yield** = 2 cocktails

Death by Chocolate Martini

As if the "martini" part isn't indulgent enough, let's dress it up with chocolate! Rich and creamy, this is not for the lightweight cocktail drinker. The Death by Chocolate Martini packs a punch with a whole lot of chocolate.

6 tablespoons (38 g) ground chocolate wafer cookies
1 tablespoon (7 g) confectioners' sugar
2 lime wedges
3 ounces (90 ml) chocolate liqueur
3 ounces (90 ml) dark crème de cacao
2 ounces (60 ml) vanilla vodka
3 ounces (90 ml) half-and-half

Combine the cookie crumbs with confectioners' sugar on a flat plate. Coat rims of two chilled martini glasses with the lime juice and then plunge rims into the cookie-crumb mixture. Set aside.

Fill a large cocktail shaker with ice and pour in the chocolate liqueur, crème de cacao, vodka, and half-and-half. Shake vigorously and strain into the glasses. Serve.

Prep = 10 minutes **Yield** = 2 cocktails

Tootsie Roll Cocktail

This has been a favorite special celebration drink among my friends for a while. Most often it shows up at our annual St. Patrick's Day event. What better day to bring out the Irish cream? Served either hot or cold, this is a great addition to your cocktail repertoire.

6   ounces (175 ml) premium vodka
2   ounces (60 ml) Irish cream liqueur (such as Bailey's)
2   ounces(60 ml) coffee liqueur (such as Kahlúa)
1   cup (235 ml) prepared hot cocoa
    Whipped cream, for garnish
    Shaved chocolate, for garnish

Fill a large cocktail shaker half full with ice cubes. Add the vodka, Irish cream, coffee liqueur, and cocoa. Shake vigorously, strain into 2 cocktail glasses, and serve. For a hot drink, pour the vodka, Irish cream, and coffee liqueur into two Irish coffee mugs, topping off with the hot cocoa. Top with whipped cream and shaved chocolate, serve.

Prep = 10 minutes   **Yield** = 2 cocktails

Chocolate Chip Cookie Cocktail

Though its name is deceptive, this is not a kids' drink—this treat is for adults only.

- 2 ounces (60 ml) vanilla vodka
- 2 ounces (60 ml) chocolate mint Irish cream
- 2 ounces (60 ml) light crème de menthe
- 1 cup (235 ml) Double Hot Chocolate (page 210)
- Whipped cream, to garnish
- Unsweetened cocoa powder, for dusting

Pour the vodka, Irish cream, and crème de menthe into a cocktail shaker, stir. Divide between two Irish coffee mugs. Add hot chocolate, dividing between the mugs. Top with whipped cream and dust with cocoa powder.

Caramel Cocoa Cocktail

Hot chocolate, which is delicious on its own, sometimes needs a little kick. With this wintertime delight in hand, cozy up next to the fire and enjoy this cocktail with a friend.

- 2 ounces (60 ml) Irish cream liqueur
- 4 ounces (120 ml) vanilla vodka
- 1 cup (235 ml) Double Hot Chocolate (page 210)
- Whipped cream, to garnish
- Ground cinnamon, to garnish

Combine irish cream and vodka in a shaker and stir. Divide between two coffee mugs and add the hot cocoa, divided between mugs. Top with whipped cream and sprinkle with ground cinnamon.

Prep = 10 minutes   **Yield** = 2 hot cocktails

Peppermint Patty Hot Drink

I bring this warming concoction out around the holidays when peppermint is most popular, though it's delicious any time of year. Try it as a nightcap after any winter holiday or celebration.

1 cup (235 ml) Double Hot Chocolate (page 210)
2 ounces (60 ml) peppermint schnapps
4 ounces (120 ml) chocolate liqueur (such as Godiva brand)
  Whipped cream, to garnish
½ ounce (15 g) bittersweet chocolate, shaved
1 peppermint candy, crushed

Combine the first three ingredients in a pitcher and pour into Irish coffee mugs. Top each with whipped cream and sprinkle with shaved chocolate and crushed peppermint candy.

Prep = 10 minutes   **Yield** = 2 hot cocktails

Double Hot Chocolate

While store-bought mixes may be a quick fix, they just don't do hot chocolate justice. Authentic hot chocolate is rich and creamy, with layers of chocolate flavor, and it requires only a few ingredients. As with all recipes, the higher quality the chocolate, the better the finished product will be. Cocoa is the star in this drink, so get the best.

- ⅓ cup (30 g) unsweetened cocoa powder
- ¾ cup (150 g) granulated sugar
- 1 teaspoon pure vanilla extract
  Pinch of salt
- ½ cup (120 ml) hot water
- 4½ cups (1 L) whole milk
- 1 ounce (28 g) dark chocolate, grated

Whisk together the cocoa powder, sugar, vanilla, salt, and hot water in a medium saucepan. Place the saucepan over medium-high heat, and add the milk, stirring to combine. Heat until steam rises, stirring occasionally. Add the grated chocolate and stir to combine. Once heated through, serve.

Prep = 15 minutes **Yield** = 5 cups (1.2 L)

Chocolate Chunk Ice Cream

Growing up, summer wasn't summer until I could hear the low hum of the ice-cream maker churning. It could not freeze quickly enough for me. This recipe is a classic: chocolate ice cream studded with chunks of even more chocolate.

2½	cups (570 ml) whole milk
12	ounces (340 g) plus 4 ounces (115 g) coarsely chopped dark chocolate
2	teaspoons pure vanilla extract
1¼	cups (250 g) granulated sugar
6	large egg yolks
3	tablespoons (18 g) unsweetened cocoa powder
2½	cups (570 ml) whipping cream
2	tablespoons (30 ml) chocolate liqueur

Heat the milk, 12 ounces (340 g) of the chocolate, vanilla, and ½ cup (100 g) sugar in a medium saucepan over medium-high heat. Bring to a boil, reduce heat, and simmer until chocolate is melted. Meanwhile, beat the egg yolks with the cocoa powder and remaining sugar until smooth and creamy. With the mixer running on low, gradually, in a steady stream, add the warm milk mixture to the eggs, slowly so as not to curdle the eggs. Pour mixture into the cleaned saucepan and place over low heat, stirring constantly with a wooden spoon until thickened and mixture coats the back of the spoon. Remove from heat and strain through a fine mesh sieve into a bowl. Add the cream and chocolate liqueur and stir to combine. Cover with plastic wrap and refrigerate for at least 4 hours and up to overnight, until chilled through. Remove from refrigerator and stir in the reserved chopped chocolate. Churn the mixture in an ice-cream machine following the manufacturer's instructions. Serve.

Variations:
Chocolate Chunk Peanut Butter: Add ¼ cup (65 g) creamy peanut butter to the mixture with the cream and chocolate liqueur.

Chocolate Chunk Brownie: Stir in 1 cup (200 g) Crumbled Brownies (page 30) with the chopped chocolate chunks just before churning.

Prep = 20 minutes **Chill** = 4 hours (includes churning)

Southern Peach and White Chocolate Ice Cream

In Austin, Texas, there is a marble slab ice-cream shop that has the most delicious ice cream. One of my favorites is white chocolate with a variety of fruits mixed in, which varies each day.

- 2 cups (400 g) peeled, pitted, and finely chopped ripe peaches
- 1/2 cup (100 g) granulated sugar, divided
- 1/4 cup (83 g) light corn syrup
- 1 1/2 cups (355 ml) half-and-half
- 1 cup (235 ml) heavy cream, divided
- 1/2 cup (120 ml) coconut milk
- 5 egg yolks
- 4 ounces (115 g) white chocolate, melted
- 1/2 cup (55 g) coarsely chopped pecans
- 1/2 teaspoon vanilla extract
- 1/2 teaspoon ground cinnamon

In a saucepan over medium heat, combine the peaches, 1/4 cup (50 g) of the sugar, and the corn syrup. Cook, stirring, until the sugar is dissolved, 3 to 5 minutes. Transfer to a large bowl and set aside.

In the same saucepan, over medium-high heat, combine the half-and-half, 1/2 cup (120 ml) of the cream, and the coconut milk; bring to a simmer and remove from the heat. In a metal bowl, whisk the egg yolks and the remaining 1/4 cup (50 g) of sugar. Gradually pour the hot cream mixture into the yolk mixture, whisking constantly. Return the mixture to the saucepan and set over medium-low heat. Cook, stirring constantly with a wooden spoon, until the custard coats the back of the spoon, 4 to 6 minutes. Do not allow to boil. Pour the custard through a fine-mesh sieve into the peach mixture. Transfer half of the mixture to a blender and puree until smooth, being careful of the hot mixture expanding out of the blender. Pour the puree into the remaining peach mixture. Add the melted white chocolate, pecans, vanilla, cinnamon, and the remaining 1/2 cup (120 ml) cream; whisk to blend. Cover and refrigerate for at least 1 hour.

Transfer the custard to an ice-cream maker and churn accordingly. Place ice cream in a freezer-safe container, and freeze at least 4 hours or up to 3 days, before serving.

Prep = 30 minutes **Yield** = About 6 cups (840 g)

Soda Fountain Chocolate Float

This recipe is a tribute to days gone by. Growing up, I could always be found at Pampelle's Soda Shop downtown. Often, I was behind the counter with my friend Emma, working the soda fountain, though I was only nine or ten years old and could barely reach the pulls. Chocolate floats were a staple, and together Emma and I made the best ones. The building is still there, though Pampelle's is long gone—but the tradition of soda fountain floats can still live on with this simple and delicious recipe.

- ½ cup (120 ml) cold club soda, plus additional to top off
- 6 tablespoons (90 ml) Chocolate Syrup (page 230)
- 4 scoops vanilla ice cream

In two tall glasses, stir together the club soda and the chocolate syrup. Add two scoops of ice cream to each glass and top off with additional club soda. Add a straw and an iced-tea spoon and serve immediately.

For a variation, use cola or root beer instead of club soda.

Prep = 5 minutes **Yield** = 2 servings

Frozen Banana Bites

Looking for a fun, nutritious afternoon treat? Bananas are a great, versatile snack, but sometimes they need a little punch. These are perfect frozen snacks for hot summer days. The toppings here are only suggestions—any candies or treats you'd like with a banana will do.

4	ripe but firm bananas
16	Popsicle sticks or thick wooden skewers
6	ounces (170 g) dark chocolate
½	cup (60 g) finely chopped pecans
½	cup (60 g) finely chopped walnuts
½	cup (35 g) flaked coconut
½	cup (50 g) finely crumbled salted pretzels
½	cup (75 g) finely crumbled ginger snaps

Peel the bananas and cut into 2-inch (5 cm) pieces (try to get four equal slices out of each banana). Stick a Popsicle stick halfway into the bottom of each banana slice. Place on a sheet pan and freeze for 1 hour. Meanwhile, melt the chocolate and set aside. Set the rest of the toppings out on plates. Remove the bananas from the freezer and dip into the chocolate, thoroughly coating and allowing any excess to drip back into the pan. Roll each banana piece in a topping, place on a waxed paper-lined sheet pan, and return to the freezer. Freeze for an additional hour, or until the chocolate and toppings are set. Serve frozen.

Prep = 20 minutes **Freeze** = 2 hours **Yield** = 16 bites

7

The Basics: Sauces, Frostings, and Glazes

Simple Chocolate Frosting

There are only two ingredients in this frosting. The trick to a creamy, smooth frosting is the blending. Beat the frosting until the desired consistency; as it cools it will set up and become more stiff and thick.

1   cup (235 ml) heavy whipping cream
12 ounces (340 g) dark chocolate chips or squares, chopped

Place chocolate in a heatproof bowl. Heat the cream in a small saucepan over medium-high heat until just steaming and bubbling. Pour cream over chocolate and let sit for 3 minutes, then use a wooden spoon to blend chocolate and cream until smooth and silky; let cool for 30 minutes. Place the frosting in the bowl of a stand mixer fitted with the paddle attachment; beat on high speed until creamy and a spreadable consistency, about 3 minutes. Use immediately or cover and refrigerate for up to 3 days. When ready to use, remove from the refrigerator and let stand for 20 minutes, until soft and spreadable.

Yield = 2½ cups (575 g), enough for 1 layer cake

Chocolate Buttercream Frosting

This simple recipe makes enough buttercream for a single 9-inch (22.5 cm) round cake (double the recipe for a larger cake). Make it ahead of time and keep covered and refrigerated until ready to use. Remove from the refrigerator 30 minutes before ready to use and let the frosting come to room temperature for easy spreading.

$1/2$ cup (45 g) premium unsweetened cocoa powder
$2^3/4$ cups (275 g) sifted confectioners' sugar
6 tablespoons (83 g) unsalted butter, softened
5 tablespoons (75 ml) whole milk
1 teaspoon pure vanilla extract

In a small bowl, whisk together the cocoa and confectioners' sugar. In the bowl of a stand mixer fitted with the paddle attachment, beat the butter with $1/2$ cup (50 g) of the cocoa mixture until smooth. Add the remaining cocoa mixture with milk and vanilla, beating to a thick, spreadable consistency.

Yield = 2 cups (500 g) frosting, enough for 1 layer cake

Chocolate Curls or Rolls

There are two ways to make chocolate curls, one having a more controlled result than the other. Both are delicious and versatile.

The simplest way: Using a block of room-temperature chocolate of your choice (the thicker the bar, the better the curl will be), pull the blade of a vegetable peeler up the side of the chocolate bar, forming a curl as it goes.

A more effective yet time-consuming way is to melt 6 ounces (170 g) of chocolate and pour onto a clean and dry marble slab or stone countertop. Using an offset pastry spreader, spread the chocolate to a thickness of $\frac{1}{8}$ inch (0.3 cm). Allow to cool completely and harden, about 1 hour. Using a stiff, wide-bladed utensil (such as a pastry scraper), push under the chocolate (like scraping your icy windshield in the winter) in one continuous motion, making curls as you go along.

Prep = Block technique, 5 minutes. Melting technique, 10 minutes
Cook = Melting technique, 5 minutes   **Yield** = Block technique, varies by size of chocolate bar. Melting technique, about 1 dozen

White Chocolate Glaze

Glazes are poured over a cake or pastry, coating in an even layer, cooling along the way. The longer the glaze cools, the thicker it becomes, making it spreadable and not necessarily pourable. Cool to the consistency you like; if you need to, you can simply reheat it in a double boiler.

1   cup (175 g) chopped white chocolate
¼   cup (60 ml) whipping cream
1   teaspoon light corn syrup
½   teaspoon brandy

In the top of a double boiler melt the chocolate. Heat the cream and corn syrup in a small saucepan until just boiling. Pour the cream over the chocolate and stir gently to combine. Set aside to cool slightly, until the mixture reaches a coating consistency. Use over cakes or brownies.

Chocolate Glaze

Chocolate glaze is fantastic for pouring over doughnuts, muffins, cupcakes, or layer cakes.

2   cups (350 g) finely chopped dark or 2¼ cups (394 g) finely chopped milk chocolate
½   cup (120 ml) whipping cream
2   teaspoons light corn syrup
1   teaspoon brandy

Melt the chocolate in the top of a double boiler. In a saucepan over medium heat, warm the cream until steam begins to rise and bubbles form around the edges. Remove the cream from the heat; add the melted chocolate, corn syrup, and brandy; stir until smooth. Allow to cool at least 30 minutes or longer, depending on its use.

Prep = 10 minutes **Chill** = At least 30 minutes, depending on use
Yield = 2½ cups (500 g), enough to glaze
a 9-inch (22.5 cm) round cake

Chocolate Ganache

Classically speaking, ganache is the base for truffles, but it is so versatile that it can be used as a filling; a glaze; and the base for tarts, soufflés, and ice creams.

Making ganache is simple, but it requires good ingredients to achieve a silky smooth finish. The smoother the chocolate, the smoother and more velvety the ganache. Depending on its intended use, ganache is prepared in many consistencies. Here you have the ratios for three different ganaches: thick, for cutting shapes and figures; velvety medium, for truffles; and soft or pouring, for glazes and ice cream and tart bases.

THICK GANACHE—FOR CUTTING AND SHAPING
- 1/2 cup (120 ml) heavy whipping cream
- 2 cups (350 g) finely chopped dark chocolate, or 1 1/2 cups (263 g) finely chopped milk chocolate, or 2 1/4 cups (394 g) finely chopped white chocolate

VELVETY GANACHE—BEST FOR TRUFFLES
- 1/2 cup (120 ml) heavy whipping cream
- 1 1/2 cups (263 g) finely chopped dark chocolate, or 1 2/3 cups (291 g) finely chopped milk chocolate, or 2 cups (350 g) finely chopped white chocolate

SOFT OR POURING GANACHE—FOR PIPING, FILLINGS, AND GLAZES
- 1/2 cup (120 ml) heavy whipping cream
- 1 1/4 cups (219 g) finely chopped dark chocolate or 1 1/3 cups (228 g) finely chopped milk chocolate, or 1 1/2 cups (263 g) finely chopped white chocolate

Place the chopped chocolate in a heatproof bowl. Heat the cream in a small saucepan over medium-high heat until just steaming and bubbling. Pour the cream over chocolate and let sit for 3 minutes, then, using a wooden spoon, stir to combine the chocolate and cream until smooth and silky. Ganache can be used in several ways; use warm as a drizzling sauce or completely cooled as a frosting. The more it cools, the stiffer it gets.

(Continued on page 230)

(Continued from page 229)

BUTTER GANACHE

Adding butter to ganache gives it a brilliant sheen.

> 3   cups (525 g) finely chopped dark chocolate
> 1½   cups (355 ml) heavy whipping cream
> 8   tablespoons (1 stick, or 112 g) unsalted butter, softened

Melt the chocolate in the top of a double boiler. In another saucepan, heat the heavy cream over medium heat just until steam begins to rise and bubbles form around the edges. Pour the melted chocolate into the cream, stirring to combine. Let the chocolate cool for 5 minutes, and then gradually, 2 tablespoons (28 g) at a time, stir in the softened butter until smooth. Allow the mixture to cool to a spreadable consistency.

Flavoring ganache is as easy as making it. By either adding extracts or emulsions to the final mixture or by steeping flavor into the cream, you can make some really interesting and elegant flavor combinations. These techniques are best used when making truffles, where a multitude of flavor possibilities exist.

Variations:

Vanilla: For a perfect vanilla flavor, infuse the heavy cream with ½ of a vanilla bean when warming it. Let steep for 15 minutes, remove the vanilla bean, reheat the cream, and add to the chocolate. Alternatively add ½ teaspoon pure vanilla extract to the heavy cream when warming.

Fruit: For a variety of fruit flavors, add ½ to 1 teaspoon of any fruit extract or emulsion to the heavy cream while warming.

Liqueurs and spirits: Rum and fruit or other liqueurs are a great way to add flavor and depth to a ganache. While the cream is warm, add 1 to 2 teaspoons of rum (light or dark-dark gives a much deeper, spicier flavor), coffee liqueur, Irish cream, cassis, orange liqueur, etc.

Coffee: In this book we have made espresso truffles with the addition of instant espresso powder. This is always a simple way of adding a coffee flavor to a recipe without increasing the liquid used. Simply dissolve instant coffee or (for a stronger flavor) espresso powder in the warming heavy cream. For these ganache recipes, 1 to 2 teaspoons, depending on your desired intensity, is plenty.

Prep = varies **Cook** = varies **Yield** = varies

Fondue

A fondue pot is the easiest way to serve a fondue, but it's not necessary. Wooden or steel skewers and any serving bowl are fine—you may just need to reheat the fondue during service. Simply place the bowl over a pot of boiling water, allowing the bowl to sit just above the water. Anything that can be coated in chocolate can serve as a dipper.

FONDUE DIPPERS:
Strawberries
Pineapple chunks
Large marshmallows
Banana slices
Shortbread cookies (page 18)
Brownie cubes (page 30)
Pound cake cubes (page 146–147)
Figs

CLASSIC CHOCOLATE FONDUE
12 ounces (340 g) premium dark chocolate, chopped
¾ cup (175 ml) heavy cream
1 teaspoon pure vanilla extract

In a small saucepan, heat the heavy cream just until steam begins to rise and bubbles form on the surface. Remove from the heat; add the chocolate, stirring to melt. Once the chocolate is melted, add the vanilla and stir. Pour the chocolate into a fondue pot or a serving dish and serve.

Prep = 10 minutes **Yield** = 4 to 6 servings

MOCHA FONDUE

- 12 ounces (340 g) premium dark chocolate, chopped
- ³⁄₄ cup (175 ml) heavy cream
- 1 tablespoon (3 g) instant espresso powder
- 2 tablespoons (30 ml) coffee liqueur

In a small saucepan, heat the heavy cream just until steam begins to rise and bubbles form on the surface. Remove from the heat and stir in the espresso powder until dissolved. Add the chocolate, stirring to melt. Once the chocolate is melted, add the coffee liqueur and stir. Pour the chocolate into a fondue pot or serving dish and serve.

CHOCOLATE-ORANGE FONDUE

- 1 cup (235 ml) heavy cream
- 2 orange-flavored herbal tea bags
- 2 large slices orange peel
- 12 ounces (340 g) premium dark chocolate, chopped

In a small saucepan over medium-high heat, combine the heavy cream with the tea bags and orange peel, heating just until steam begins to rise and bubbles form on the surface. Remove from the heat, cover, and steep for about 30 minutes. Remove the orange peel and tea bags, wringing out any liquid. Reheat the cream until steam begins to rise. Turn off the heat and add the chocolate, stirring until melted. Pour the chocolate into a fondue pot or serving dish and serve.

CHOCOLATE PEANUT BUTTER FONDUE

- 1¼ cups (295 ml) light cream
- 6 ounces (170 g) unsweetened dark chocolate, chopped
- ½ cup (100 g) granulated sugar
- ⅓ cup (87 g) creamy peanut butter
- 1½ teaspoons pure vanilla extract

In a small saucepan, heat the cream just until steam begins to rise and bubbles form on the surface. Remove from the heat and stir in the chocolate and sugar. Once the chocolate is melted, add the peanut butter and vanilla, stirring to combine. Pour the chocolate into a fondue pot or serving dish and serve.

Chocolate Fudge Frosting

This differs from other chocolate frostings because it has a few more ingredients, making it a rich, decadent frosting with the taste of creamy chocolate fudge. Use this on any number of cakes and brownies as an elegant finish.

1¼ cups (285 g) firmly packed light brown sugar
¼ cup (23 g) premium unsweetened cocoa powder
3 tablespoons (42 g) shortening
2 tablespoons (28 g) unsalted butter
¼ teaspoon salt
½ cup (120 ml) whole milk
1½ cups (150 g) sifted confectioners' sugar
1 teaspoon pure vanilla extract

Combine brown sugar, cocoa, shortening, butter, salt, and milk in a medium saucepan. Cook over medium heat, stirring constantly, until the mixture comes to a boil, then boil for 3 minutes. Remove from heat and let cool. Using a hand mixer or a stand mixer fitted with the paddle attachment; beat the cocoa mixture with the confectioners' sugar and vanilla until smooth and spreadable, adding additional milk if necessary. Spread on cake immediately.

Yield = About 3 cups (675 g), enough for a 2-layer cake

White Chocolate Cream Cheese Frosting

Cream cheese frosting on any cake makes it a success. Try this frosting on any of your favorite cakes and bars.

- 5 ounces (140 g) white chocolate
- 16 ounces (455 g) cream cheese, softened
- 8 tablespoons (1 stick, or 112 g) unsalted butter, softened
- 4 cups (400 g) confectioners' sugar
- $3/4$ teaspoons rum extract (or dark or spiced rum)

Melt the chocolate in the top of a double boiler and set aside. In the bowl of a stand mixer fitted with the paddle attachment, beat the cream cheese and butter until smooth. Add 2 cups of the powdered sugar and beat on low until blended. Add the melted chocolate, remaining 2 cups powdered sugar, and rum; blend on low speed until just combined. Turn the mixer to high, and beat the frosting until creamy and smooth, about 2 minutes.

Yield = 3 cups (900 g), enough for a multilayer cake

Chocolate Syrup

For chocolate milk, ice cream, enticing adult cocktails, or just to drizzle over anything, this syrup is a must for your refrigerator.

1 cup (200 g) granulated sugar
1 cup (235 ml) water
8 ounces (225 g) premium dark chocolate

Combine the sugar and water in a saucepan over medium heat. Heat until the sugar is dissolved. Add the chocolate and stir to melt and blend. Remove and cool completely. Place in a jar and refrigerate until needed.

Prep = 15 minutes **Chill** = At least 2 hours
Yield = 2 1/2 cups (570 ml)

Chocolate Yum Yum Filling

This delicious recipe is a filling for cannoli, trifles, cookie sandwiches, layer cakes, and more.

4 ounces (115 g) unsweetened chocolate
1 cup (2 sticks, or 225 g) unsalted butter, softened
1 cup (200 g) granulated sugar
2 teaspoons pure vanilla extract
6 large eggs

Melt the chocolate in the top of a double boiler and set aside. In the bowl of a stand mixer fitted with the paddle attachment, cream the butter with the sugar until light and fluffy. Beat in the melted chocolate and vanilla. Add the eggs one at a time, beating for 2 minutes after each addition. Beat until the sugar is dissolved, then chill.

Prep = 15 minutes
Yield = About 2 1/2 cups (660 g) filling

Chocolate Dipped Everything

For dipping everything from pretzels to strawberries, bananas to dried fruit, this is chocolate dessert at its simplest. This is enough melted chocolate for 1 pound (455 g) of chocolate-dipped strawberries with white chocolate for decorative striping.

8   ounces (225 g) premium dark chocolate, chopped
4   ounces (115 g) white chocolate, chopped

Line a baking sheet with parchment paper or waxed paper. Wash the strawberries or other fruit if the skin will be eaten and dry well. Prepare two separate double boilers, and melt dark chocolate in the top of one and white chocolate in the top of the other. Working with well-dried fruit, dip in dark chocolate, twisting and plunging to cover. Place on a parchment-lined sheet pan and allow to cool until set, about 30 minutes. Dip a fork in the white chocolate and drizzle in a stream over the chocolate-covered fruit. Alternatively, pour white chocolate into a resealable plastic bag and snip off one of the corners. Pipe the white chocolate over the chocolate-dipped fruit.

Prep = 10 minutes   **Cook** = 1 hour
Yield = About 12 chocolate-dipped strawberries

Index

Note: Page numbers in italics indicate photographs.

S

sage, 154, 194
Salad of Asiago Pepper Crisps with Cocoa Nibs and Beets, 162–163
salads
 Apple Slaw, 178–179
 Pear and Walnut Salad, 160
 Salad of Asiago Pepper Crisps with Cocoa Nibs and Beets, 162–163
Salt and Pepper Sugar Topping, 166–167
Salt-Roasted Shrimp with White Chocolate Balsamic Dipping Sauce, 191
sauces, 216. *See also* moles
 Chocolate Balsamic Sauce, 190
 Chocolate Barbecue Sauce, 158
 Chocolate Cherry Port Sauce, 159
 Chocolate Island Sauce, 177
 White Chocolate Balsamic Dipping Sauce, 191
savory items, 151–195
scallions, 192
scallops, 190
Scharffen Berger, 10
scones, 77
semisweet chocolate, 9
sesame seeds, 63
sesame sticks, 157
shortbread, 18–19, 100–101, 102–103, 226
shrimp, 191, 192
Shrimp with Scallion and Chocolate-Balsamic Sauce, 192, *193*
Simple Chocolate Frosting, 217
single-origin chocolates, 11
single-plantation chocolates, 11
slaw, 178–179
Slow-Roasted Cocoa Pepper Pork Tenderloin, 180
smoothies, 197
 Berry Blast Smoothie, 200
 Chocolate Morning Smoothie, 198, *199*
snack mix, 157
Snow-Capped Canyon Cookies, 54, *55*
Soda Fountain Chocolate Float, 214
Soft Ganache, 223
soufflés
Mocha Hazelnut Chocolate Soufflé, 108
Sweet Potato-White Chocolate Soufflé, 166–167
soups. *See* chilis
sour cream, 67
Sour Cream Double-Chocolate Muffins, 68, *69*
Southern Peach and White Chocolate Ice Cream, 213

Spiced Nuts with Cocoa Nibs and Chocolate Chips, 156
sticky buns, 74–76
St. Joseph's Day Pastries, 28
strawberries, 63, 84, 200, 226
streusel, 134–135
sugar, 7
sunflower seeds, 157
sweet potatoes, 134–135, 166–167
Sweet Potato-White Chocolate Soufflé, 166–167
Sweet S'Mores French Toast, 64, *65*
syrups
 Chocolate Syrup, 230
 Coffee Syrup, 130–132

T

tacos, 173
Tanzania, 7
tarts, 80–111
 Caramel Peanut Butter Tart with Salted Almond Crust, 92–93
 Truffle Tart with Shortbread Crust, 100–101
 White Chocolate Cherry Tart with Shortbread Crust, 102–103
tassies, 45
Thick Ganache, 223
Three-Bean Beef Chili, 172
Three-Pepper Grating Chocolate, 153
Toasted Coconut-Chocolate Chunk Pecan Pie, 96–98, *97*
toffee, 43
Tootsie Roll Cocktail, 206, *207*
toppings. *See also* frostings; ganaches; glazes; sauces; syrups
 Chocolate Curls or Rolls, 220
 Salt and Pepper Sugar Topping, 166–167
tortes, 112–150
trifles, 84, 85
Trinitario cacao trees, 7
Triple Chocolate Pecan Clusters, 22
truffles (candies), 100–101
 Classic Chocolate Truffles, 24–25, *25*
 Espresso-Nut Truffles, *25*
 Green Tea Truffles with Bay Essence, 27
 Raspberry Pecan Truffles, 23
truffles (fungi), 164
Truffle Tart with Shortbread Crust, 100–101
turnovers, 70
turtles, 39
Twice-Baked Truffle Mashed Potatoes with White Chocolate, 164, *165*

About the Author

Dwayne Ridgaway, a native of Kerrville, Texas, lives in Bristol, Rhode Island. He is author of seven books including *Lasagna: The Art of Layered Cooking; Pizza: 50 Traditional and Alternative Recipes for the Oven and the Grill;* and *Cast Iron Cooking: 50 Gourmet-Quality Dishes from Entrees to Desserts.* Dwayne is a graduate of Johnson and Wales University, and currently works as a food and beverage consultant, project manager, caterer, and event designer. He has made a career out of exploring and celebrating the culinary arts. His passion drives him to develop fresh and unique recipes that any reader can execute and enjoy. Dwayne's goal continues to be for all readers to use his recipes and writing as a groundwork for their own personal creativity.

Acknowledgments

There are as many ways to cook with chocolate as there are people to create a cookbook on the subject. Editors, proof readers, photographers, designers, and stylists spend endless hours to make such a beautiful thing happen.

I owe this project to Rochelle Bourgault, my editor, and Winnie Prentiss, my publisher, who offered me this opportunity. Thank you both for the years of support and dedication.

Many thanks to Sandy Smith, copy editor and recipe tester, for your numerous hours of attention. To Glenn Scott, photographer, who brought my words to life, and to Catrine Kelty, the food stylist, whose job is no cake walk. To Betsy Gammons, project manager, for keeping me on schedule during the development of this book.

There are a few people that contributed to my development of recipes that I would like to thank. Johnny McGovern and Cliff and Kathy McGovern, thank you so much for your lessons, palates, and honesty. To Johnny, a special thanks to you for sharing some of your time-honored bake shop recipes. Thank you to my mother, who opened her recipe drawer and offered her advice. As always, thanks to all of my friends and family who support me along the way—especially to Tony who puts up with a house in complete disarray when I'm writing and yet remains my biggest fan!

Thank you to all the readers who have bought this book—enjoy!